Beautiful in God's Eyes
for Young Women

ELIZABETH GEORGE

HARVEST HOUSE PUBLISHERS
EUGENE, OREGON

Cover by Dugan Design Group, Bloomington, Minnesota

BEAUTIFUL IN GOD'S EYES FOR YOUNG WOMEN
Copyright © 2014 by Elizabeth George
Published by Harvest House Publishers
Eugene, Oregon 97402
www.harvesthousepublishers.com

Library of Congress Cataloging-in-Publication Data
   George, Elizabeth, 1944-
   Beautiful in God's eyes for young women / Elizabeth George.
      pages cm
   Includes bibliographical references.
   ISBN 978-0-7369-2855-7 (pbk.)
   ISBN 978-0-7369-5522-5 (eBook)
   1. Teenage girls—Religious life. 2. Christian teenagers—Religious life. 3. Bible. Proverbs, XXXI, 10-31—Criticism, interpretation, etc. I. Title.
   BV4551.3.G44 2014
   248.8'33—dc23

                                     2013034393

This book is lovingly dedicated to
all the "girls" in my life:

To my daughter Katherine,
and her daughter Taylor
To my daughter Courtney,
and her daughters Katie, Grace, and Lily

I thank God for each of you and your beautiful hearts
every day of my life.

Contents

A Word of Welcome

Dear precious friend,

As a young woman, I'm sure you think every day about how you look, what's in and what's out of fashion, and who's cool and who isn't. Daily life as a girl of any age can be a struggle when you don't know what to do, how to act, and what's important.

Well, welcome to this exciting book about beauty—true beauty, authentic beauty. I've entitled it *Beautiful in God's Eyes for Young Women* because it tells you once and for all exactly what God says is important in life, and exactly what is beautiful in His eyes. If you have a relationship with God through His Son, Jesus Christ, guess what? You *are* beautiful in God's eyes. Nothing and no one, and no fads or popular people or trends can ever change how God sees you. *He* has made you beautiful in Him.

As you go through this book featuring Proverbs 31:10-31, you will discover character traits that you can grow in and nurture in your life to be beautiful inside and out, qualities that honor the Lord and bless others. No matter how old you become, and no matter how your life circumstances change— whether you marry or not, whether you have children or not—these character traits stand forever as God's will and purpose and plan for you every single day of your life.

So grab a friend—or two! Get some copies of this book to share. Together, go on the life-changing journey and beauty makeover God provides in His Word, the Bible. You'll see your confidence bloom. You'll discover your personal talents and abilities and how to develop them. And you'll feel your heart expand as you step outside of yourself and extend mercy and goodness and a helping hand to those in need, beginning right in your own home.

And best of all? You will reap the priceless reward of knowing God is pleased, of knowing what the right thing to do is... and doing it. No one can put a value on this kind of confidence—confidence in the Lord as you walk closely with Him.

As you study, I'll be praying for you. I'm already so proud of you in the Lord just because you desire to be even more beautiful in His eyes!

In His great and amazing love,

Your friend and sister in Christ,

Elizabeth George

1

A Sparkling Jewel

Your Value

"Who can find a virtuous woman?
For her price is far above rubies."

PROVERBS 31:10 (KJV)

*I*t was a dream come true. I was finally going to meet her! I'm talking about the woman in Proverbs 31, a woman who was so beautiful in God's eyes. She's the woman we'll be getting to know throughout this book. And the only reason I was on my way to see where she lived in Israel was because my husband, Jim, was taking a group of seminary students to Israel for a study course. I'm still so thankful he invited me to come along!

You see, Jim knew. He knew that for 20 years I'd done everything I could to learn about this incredible woman. He knew I had memorized many versions of this Bible passage in Proverbs 31:10-31.

From our credit card account he also knew that I had made her life a personal study project for that same 20-year span.

11

Yes, I had invested heavily in a library of books about the book of Proverbs...and especially about this woman in chapter 31.

Jim knew that knowing as much as I could about her was a lifetime goal of mine. Yes, he definitely knew what meeting her would mean to me. As I said, a trip to her homeland? To meet the Proverbs 31 woman? That was indeed a dream come true!

But before heading off to Israel, I made a list of "Things to See." I noted every cultural element of Proverbs 31:10-31 that I wanted to see for myself in Israel. Oh yeah, I was on a mission! "Who can find a virtuous woman?" Proverbs 31:10 asks. Well, I was going to find her!

An Alphabet of Character

Where, you might wonder, did this woman come from? And how did the woman in Proverbs 31 become a standard for beauty the way God sees it? Believe it or not, she began with a real flesh-and-blood woman!

Once upon a time there was a young prince who would someday be king. He had many lessons to learn before he took the throne. So his mother often sat down with him and taught him how to be a godly king, and also how to find an outstanding wife.

Most Bible scholars agree that Proverbs 31 contains that wise mother's instruction to her young son. Verse 1 says, "These are the wise sayings of King Lemuel...taught to him at his mother's knee" (TLB). In verses 1-9 she covers the basics of leadership. Then she moves on in verses 10-31 and describes the kind of woman he should marry. This woman would indeed be a rare treasure.

But the prince's mom didn't just *tell* him. She *taught* him in a way he wouldn't forget. She organized the list of qualities he was to look for in a wife according to the letters of the Hebrew alphabet. Each quality began with a letter of the Hebrew alphabet. We would say that she taught him the ABCs of finding a godly wife. Presented in this simple way, this alphabet of feminine character could be quickly learned, easily remembered and memorized, regularly recited, and permanently etched into the young boy's heart.

Searching for Treasure

As you read about the Proverbs 31 woman in this book, you will sit alongside her and learn from her. You'll listen as she teaches you about true beauty from God's perspective. And what's the first thing you learn about an excellent, noble woman? "She is worth far more than rubies" (Proverbs 31:10). Her lesson begins by stressing what an extraordinary and exceptional treasure a truly godly woman is.

Now, let me share with you you what I found on my personal treasure hunt in Israel. First I have to tell you that my list of "Things to See" had "jewels" right at the top. I wanted to see a sample of the jewels that were used to speak of the qualities of this remarkable woman.

Wouldn't you think I would find my evidence in a place that houses crown jewels, a place like the Tower of London in England? Well, so did I. But there was no such official place. So when our study group spent a day in the Israel Museum in Jerusalem, I dashed in with my list in hand and began searching for *ITEM #1: JEWELS*.

On and on the museum's displays went. And on and on

my search for jewels continued. Covering every hall, I found not a single jewel! The jewels—along with every other item of value—had been carried away by conquering armies in days gone by.

But what I *did* find in the museum was as telling as what I didn't find. The relics in the many halls gave me clues into the kind of life lived by this woman in Proverbs 31 and other women like her. I feasted my eyes on...bones and coffins! Walls were covered with shields and swords, body armor, and instruments of war. Glass cases displayed dishes and cookware made out of...mud! Stone olive presses and millstones for grinding grains by hand were also on display. These were not at all what I had expected.

What lessons did these primitive items offer? They were a voice that spoke of hard times—of struggling to survive, of eking out a living, of barely managing to exist. These items spoke of work and war, labor and loss. There was little—if any—beauty, color, or evidence of pleasure and ease. Everything I saw was stark, bleak, and basic, testifying to a life that was stark, bleak, and basic.

Then it hit me. I suddenly realized that God's Proverbs 31 woman *was* the sparkling jewel in her husband's life. *She* brought the love, the color, the joy, the life, and the energy to her family's home.

Yes, life was bleak in Israel. And everyday life focused on just surviving in that dry, rugged land. Food, clothing, and shelter were all-consuming daily concerns. But with a wife who was a sparkling jewel, a man and his family would find such a hard life bearable. In fact, with God's beautiful woman beside him, he possessed treasure untold.

How to Be Beautiful—Inside and Out

Life is a struggle for everyone regardless of age, right? I'm sure you struggle daily to manage all that your life entails. But you have the ability and grace to bring beauty and joy into the lives of those under your roof—that is, if you want to and choose to. I'm guessing you probably don't have a husband and children. But you do have a mom and dad and brothers and sisters. You—yes, you—can light up the lives of the people at home as you share the sparkle God puts in your heart no matter how hard times are.

I hope you're catching a vision of your life as a glittering jewel, a ruby, a gemstone. As you and the members of your family face hardship, pain, weariness, drudgery, or sorrow, you have the power, through God, to help lighten their suffering. All you have to do is Step #1—want to do it; Step #2—grow in godly character; and Step #3—do it. Give your strength away every single day.

It's a fact that gems increase in value as time passes. And the same is true of you and your beautiful, Christlike character. You are one of God's excellent young women—one of His precious and priceless jewels. So let the improvements begin! Here are two exercises to help you polish up your sparkle and brighten up your life as well as the lives of those around you.

#1. Develop practical skills—As a young single, you need to sharpen the skills necessary for managing your room at home or your dorm room at college. These practical skills may not make much sense right now, but they will most definitely come in handy at some time in the future. For instance:

Homemaking—I still remember the sad tears of a soon-to-be-married college student whose mother had financed swimming lessons, encouraged her athletic efforts, and driven her to swimming pools, swim practice, and swim meets for 20 years. My friend could swim—but she couldn't cook, clean, or do her laundry!

Right now, the idea of "homemaking" may seem a little unnecessary. But one day you will have your own place (and maybe even a husband and baby). That place will become your home, and what people see there will be a reflection of who you are.

Money management—All through your life, and even today, you'll need a working knowledge of personal finances. Even if the only money you manage now is your allowance, you still need to know about wise money management—making money, saving money, giving money, and spending money.

As you work your way through Proverbs 31:10-31, you'll notice again and again the keen business head on this woman's shoulders.

Time management—The careful management of your time is key to running your life well. Time is yours to be managed every minute of every day. It's a precious commodity God gives you. And He expects you to redeem it and use it for His purposes. You'll want to become an expert in the daily habit of planning and scheduling. And you'll be so glad you did!

#2. Growing in emotional stability—To be a sparkling jewel and a blessing in anyone's life, you'll want to grow in emotional stability. After all, you are a part of your family. That

means you contribute to the general emotional atmosphere in your home. Are you an emotional train wreck at home? How about with your friends at school? How much better it is to be a positive calming influence—to be a tower of strength to those in your presence.

If you start building greater emotional stability in just a few important areas, you will make incredible progress.

First up is *master your tolerance*. This refers to endurance—endurance during tough and trying days. Everyone, including you, faces difficult circumstances and painful times. It's a fact of life. James wrote in James 1:2, "Count it all joy when you fall into various trials" (NKJV).

When trials come, don't be surprised. And don't be caught off guard without a plan for some stability. Turn to God right away. He's your helper through thick and thin. Pray something like this: "God, Your Word says I can do all things—including handle this—through Christ, who strengthens me. By Your grace and through Your Spirit, I can do this. Thank You for enabling me to meet and handle this challenge."

Next up is *master your temper*. How? Try some sure advice from God. A woman of strength:

— nurtures a peaceful heart

— knows how to wait

— does not strive

— restrains her spirit[1]

Does this sound like the impossible dream? It's not. Remember—you can do all things through Christ (Philippians 4:13).

And finally is *master your tongue*. Oh dear—we knew this was coming! Your words can either "speak like the piercings of a sword" or promote health (Proverbs 12:18 NKJV). To bring the sparkle of God's beauty to others,

— speak less often

— speak only after you think about what you're going to say

— speak only what is sweet and pleasant

— speak only what is wise and kind[2]

Now, with all these wonderful traits on track, you have soooo much to give to others at home, at school, at church, in all your activities, and with all your friends. And best of all? You give God honor and glory as you reflect His presence in you.

An Invitation to Beauty

Gems are hard stones, and these rough, hard stones need to be cut and all the flaws removed. Once cut, they are polished to add to their luster and increase their brilliance, to allow color to shine through, and to create "fire" or a rainbow-like sparkle.

Your "fire" and *your* sparkle comes by such a process too. Your character flaws are removed as you work to eliminate what is not pleasing to God, all that hurts and harms others. And as you polish up your practical skills and gain greater emotional stability, you will indeed sparkle as you bless others and shine with God's brand of beauty.

Study Questions

Using your Bible, read through Proverbs 31:10-31. Then
write out verse 10 here:

A wife of noble character who can find?
She is worth far more than rubies.

In your Bible, look at these verses and share their key
messages to you.

Homemaking

Proverbs 24:3-4—
By wisdom a house is built, and through
understanding it is established; through
knowledge its rooms are filled with rare &
beautiful treasures.

Proverbs 31:27—
She watches over the affairs of her household
and does not eat the bread of idleness.

Time Management

Colossians 4:5—
Be wise in the way you act toward
outsiders; make the most of every
opportunity.

Ephesians 2:10—
For we are God's handiwork, created
in Christ Jesus to do good works, which
God prepared in advance for us to do.

Psalm 90:12—
Teach us to number our days, that we may gain a heart of wisdom.

Emotional Stability

Tolerance: Proverbs 19:11—
A person's wisdom yields patience; it is to one's glory to overlook an offense.

Temper: Ecclesiastes 7:9—
Do not be quickly provoked in your spirit, for anger resides in the lap of fools.

Tongue: Proverbs 10:19—
Sin is not ended by multiplying words, but the prudent hold their tongues.

What was the most exciting truth or information you discovered in this chapter?

I am worth something. I have value. Gemstones need to be cut and shaped and have flaws removed and that is exactly what I need.

How did this chapter challenge you to develop godly character?

Because of where I am in my life, it is time that I become a Proverbs 31 woman and to have a relationship with Christ.

2

A Solid Rock

Your Loyalty

*"The heart of her husband trusts in her,
and he will have no lack of gain."*

*A*re you wondering as you read the verse above, *What in the world does this have to do with me? I'm not married, so clearly I don't have a husband. What's going on here?*

You are right to wonder. And yes, Proverbs 31:11 does have to do with blessing and bettering a husband's life. Granted, that will probably be you one day in the future. But what about today?

Our primary goal in this book is first and foremost to look at Proverbs 31:10-31 one verse at a time. We need to get the full picture of God's excellent woman and her many rich character traits, her virtues. Why? Because this is a key passage for every Christian woman, young or old, single or married. It is filled with wisdom that will help you through every day of your life as a woman. It is God's portrait of what a woman of excellence looks like, what she does, and how she acts…and what you want to be.

Our second goal is to make practical applications and put God's wisdom to work in your life today, to apply it right now. When you put these truths and traits to work for you, you will grow into who God wants you to become. And you'll be preparing yourself for your future, whether you marry or not. You see, it's the character qualities of this woman that count. And they count today. And they will carry you through all of life.

Like a Rock

You probably already know some things about loyalty and trust. Unfortunately our first lessons in these two character traits are usually hard ones—you know, the negative kind. For instance, all kids in the process of growing up jeopardize, at one time or another, their parents' trust. They get caught in a lie. Or they fail to keep their word. Or miss their curfew. Or deliberately break one of the rules their parents set for them.

But your goal as a young woman desiring God's list of character qualities is to be trustworthy and loyal. When this becomes one of your bedrock, nonnegotiable character traits, you will please the Lord. And you'll please your parents. You will be laying a rock-solid foundation for trust and loyalty in all your relationships with friends—and, maybe even a husband in the future.

Speaking of rocks and foundations, believe me, after studying in Israel and living in Jerusalem for three weeks, I have learned a lot about rocks! Climbing through the hill country day after day meant taking on the characteristics of a gazelle as we walked up, over, around, between, and back down the rocks.

But the most exciting rock I saw was a cornerstone. To be

more specific, it was the cornerstone at the excavated base of the south end of the Temple Mount, the site of Herod's Temple, the place where Jesus worshipped long ago.

I was thrilled to have my picture taken while leaning up against this gigantic block of stone. It supported the massive foundation of the Temple, and has sustained the weight of the 75-foot-high stone walls for more than 2000 years. It was 20 feet long, the standard height-of-a-man high (6 feet), and at least 8 feet across. Today, it still holds the weight of the entire Temple wall.

Why was I so obsessed with this cornerstone? Because that's how God speaks of His women—as "pillars" or "corner stones." In Psalm 144, David prayed for victory over his enemies. Why? He asked God this so that "our daughters will be like pillars [or 'corner stones,' KJV] carved to adorn a palace" (verse 12).

Like that wall, your character can be strengthened as you, my younger sister in the Lord, become—by His grace—a virtuous woman of strength who stands steady as a rock. The cornerstone in my picture wasn't the most beautiful thing you have ever seen. And most of it was still buried and out of sight. But its function made Herod's Temple a sight to behold!

I want you to carry this image of a cornerstone with you through this chapter because the picture of a woman—our P31 woman—standing as steady and strong as a rock is at the very heart of Proverbs 31.

The Language of Loyalty and Trust

I thought I knew all about trust, but I have to admit I found two surprises as I studied the statement "the heart of her husband safely trusts her" (Proverbs 31:11 NKJV). These surprises taught me about the importance of being a rock to my husband Jim and to all other people. But these two princi-ples of trust also apply to you as a young woman living with your parents and as you associate with friends at school and church and on a job, even if that job is babysitting or walking the neighbor's dog.

Rest—First consider "the heart"—in this case, the heart of a husband. In this passage, the Hebrew word translated "heart" refers to the mind, where doubt, anxiety, and restlessness are born and grow. But the heart or mind of a husband who trusts his wife is a heart at rest.

For you, you need to be concerned about the heart or mind of each of your parents and siblings and friends. Can they trust you? Are their hearts at ease? Their hearts are at rest whenever they know they can trust you in all things.

Your calling as one of God's young women is to live in such a solid way that others never worry or wonder about your character. They can trust your word. They can be con-fident you will follow through on whatever they ask of you. They can trust you not to talk with others about your fam-ily members or personal problems because of your loyalty. At this stage, let's hope and pray your parents, your brothers and sisters, and your friends can truly trust you and count on your loyalty.

Encouragement—Next came Surprise #2—the trust fac-tor: "The heart of her husband safely *trusts* her." The Hebrew word translated "trust" means "to be of good courage, to take heart and to feel confidence."[1] Therefore, a man married to one of God's beautiful-on-the-inside women feels confident. He is encouraged by his ability to trust in his wife![2] Put another way, her loyalty is a daily ministry of encouragement to him. Because of his confidence in her (he "safely trusts *her*"), he is encouraged and strengthened to handle all his responsibilities.

Now think about yourself as a young woman. Your calling as God's woman is to create trust in others. You want people to know they can trust you. And this starts with your parents. You encourage your parents when they know that they can trust you to speak the truth, to be where you're supposed to be, doing what you should be doing. That's what builds their confidence in you.

The Lack of Worry

As much I marveled at these first two surprises—rest and encouragement—I was actually shocked by the second half of verse 11: "So he will have no lack of gain" (NKJV). Or as the NIV says, he "lacks nothing of value."

During the time that the book of Proverbs was written (at least 3000 years ago), married women generally didn't have jobs outside the home. They had little or no formal education. And they were expected to take care of a home, take care of their husbands, and raise and take care of their children. So you can understand my surprise when I read that this woman's husband had "no lack of gain." In other words, he would never have to worry about his family's financial security.

Like me, you might be wondering, *What part could this woman play in contributing to the financial welfare of her family?* Read on!

The word "gain" comes from the cultural setting of the

book of Proverbs. At that time all those thousands of years ago, when one army defeated another, the victorious ruler and his soldiers carried off the spoils of war. These spoils were the prizes of war and comprised wealth in a time when there was no coinage. Because of the efforts of the soldiers and their superior abilities in battle, they and their families were well supplied with provisions—meaning they had no lack of gain.

The woman from Proverbs 31 is like a victorious soldier. She determined that by her personal efforts, she would contribute to her husband's finances, making sure he never lacked for anything.

This may sound crass, even unspiritual, and quite unbeautiful, but much of Proverbs 31:10-31 deals with money. God's 22-verse summary of His beautiful woman clearly shows her daily involvement in managing, making, and multiplying money. Maybe you're questioning right now why money management is so important in God's eyes, and why learning about it is a good exercise for you.

You'll get your answers about the management of money in the chapters to come. The verses to come will open your eyes to understand how valuable this discipline is—to you and your family. But for a little preview, here are a few of the reasons money matters to God.

God is honored—This teaching from Proverbs 31 about family finances—about making, managing, and multiplying money—is God's design for His women. He is honored when you follow His plan.

Your family is blessed—Even as a young woman, money management is a ministry to your family as they see day after day they can trust you with money. Let's hope they can even trust you with the family car when you are old enough to drive.

Sure, your parents oversee the family finances in a general way. But you are the one who runs a good part of your life. You also manage your own personal money on a day-to-day basis. Why, you could easily manage to spend every last cent you receive from allowances, babysitting, and birthdays on yourself!

Or you can start saving for college, for Bible camp, for a myriad of other expenses that make up a busy, exciting teen's lifestyle. The practice of spending everything on yourself benefits only you. But the practice of saving for your future goals benefits your family.

Your character grows—Proverbs 31 makes it clear that, in God's eyes, wise money management is a virtue. And so is self-control in the area of money. God wants you to nurture these twin character qualities, to grow in wisdom *and* self-control. And here's a hint: If you're going to save money, usually the one person you have to especially watch is yourself! After all, every decision *not* to spend money is money saved.

When you learn to do without, when you learn to say no, when you learn to wait, you reap great rewards. Your savings grow, your expenses fall, and your bank account builds— all of which motivates you to continue your wise money management.

Now let's talk about trust. This woman's husband trusted her. She was a solid rock to him because she could be trusted. And guess what? You can be a solid rock as well. Here are a few basic foundational attitudes and actions that build character in you and earn trust from others.

How to Be Beautiful—Inside and Out

1. Take trust seriously—God says "a virtuous woman"—a woman who's faithful, a girl who's loyal—can be trusted. The best way to begin laying this cornerstone of godly beauty is to place it at the top of your daily prayer list. Ask God to transform your character, to help you be trustworthy and loyal.

2. Keep your word—I remember listening to some college women share prayer requests at their weekly Bible study in our home. They earnestly wanted others to pray that they would become "women of their word," women who were true to their word. That's a good goal, isn't it? So challenge yourself to do what you say you'll do, be where you say you'll be, and keep the appointments you make.

3. Follow through on instructions—The degree to which you follow through on instructions is a measure of your faithfulness and loyalty. Don't be like Eve, who failed her husband—and God—when she didn't follow the Lord's guidelines regarding the tree of the knowledge of good and evil and chose to eat the forbidden fruit (Genesis 2:17; 3:1-6).

4. When in doubt, check it out!—There are lots of times when you will be pressured to make a decision. If you are not sure what is the right thing to do, don't charge into something that you will regret later. Be smart. When in doubt, check it out. Call or talk to your parents and get their input. Do the wise thing and don't be a fool. Proverbs 28:26 says, "He who trusts in his own heart is a fool" (NKJV).

5. Be accountable—When Jim and I were teaching our teen daughters about accountability and trustworthiness, we let them leave the house only after they let us know what their plans were, where they would be, who they would be with, and agreed to check in if their plans changed.

Your parents should know where you are at all times. Keeping them informed speaks loudly of your willingness to be accountable to them.

6. *Bone up on money management*—Ask your mom and dad to teach you about handling your personal finances well. Maybe you can even do what I did and take a class at school on managing your finances. I learned how to write checks, balance a checkbook, and what to watch out for when using a credit card. Learn what others are saying and doing to manage, earn, and save money.

An Invitation to Beauty

I entitled this chapter "A Solid Rock." Doesn't sound very beautiful, does it? But I want you to revisit Psalm 144:12. Here is David's prayer to God. He asked that his enemies be defeated so that "our daughters will be like pillars carved to adorn a palace."

Here's the word picture from this description: Large stone palaces were held up and supported by ornately carved pillars. Each pillar was a wonder due to its breathtaking beauty. Yet underneath the artwork was solid rock. That's you, my friend! Powerful, yet lovely.

Growing in character makes you strong and solid. Your character causes you to hold up under pressure. When you are like a stone pillar, others can depend on you, lean on you, count on you. And the traits of loyalty and trustworthiness are so beautiful that when you display them, you become a living, breathing, magnificent tribute to God.

Study Questions

Using your Bible, read through Proverbs 31:10-31. Then write out verse 11 here:

Her husband has full confidence in her and lacks nothing of value.

One hindrance to being known as a trustworthy person is lying. What do these scriptures tell you about lying?

Psalm 34:12-13— Whoever of you loves life and desires to see many good days, keep your tongue from evil and your lips from telling lies.

Proverbs 12:22— The Lord detests lying lips, but he delights in people who are trustworthy.

Proverbs 19:5— A false witness will not go unpunished, and whoever pours out lies will not go free.

In this chapter, the statement was made that "much of Proverbs 31:10-31 deals with money. God's 22-verse summary of His beautiful woman clearly shows her daily involvement in managing, making, and multiplying money." Look in your Bible at the following verses from

Proverbs 31:10-31. Then jot down how the Proverbs 31 woman managed money and resources.

Verse 13—
She selects wool & flax and works w/ eager hands.

willing & wise

Verse 14—
She is like merchant ships, bringing her food from afar.

Verse 16— ℃.
She considers a field and buys it; out of her earnings, she plants a vineyard.
thinks before purchase & uses it wisely

Verse 18—
She sees that her trading is profitable, and her lamp does not go out at night.

Verse 24—
She makes linen garments & sells them, and supplies the merchants with sashes.

Verse 27—
She watches over the affairs of her household and does not eat the bread of idleness.

Verse 31—
Honor her for all that her hands have done, and let her works bring her praise at the city gate.

What was the most exciting truth or information you discovered in this chapter?

I am capable of being a cornerstone.

How did this chapter challenge you to be more trust-worthy in character and in managing your money?

My trustworthiness not only affects my future husband and ppl I come into contact with, but it helps them to be at ease because they know they can count on me.

3

A Spring of Goodness

Your Mission

*"She does him good and not evil
all the days of her life."*

Proverbs 31:12 (nkjv)

As I'm sitting at my desk writing a chapter about God's beautiful Proverbs 31 woman who does "him"—her husband—good all the days of her life, I'm hoping I don't lose you as a reader! It's true this verse is describing a wife who's devoted to her husband, who does him good and not evil. But I'm thinking that you are probably not married. That means the "hims" in your life at this time include God Himself and your dad.

So I've come up with a double goal for this chapter and this scripture. First, I want us to explore what the verse is saying about being a wife. One day in the future, marriage and being a wife may well be true of you.

But until then, I want us to see how this woman's beautiful trait of goodness applies to you in all your relationships. All of life, and every person who crosses your path each day, presents opportunity after opportunity for you to do "good and not evil."

Pictures of Good and Evil

I've decided to christen this chapter with the title "A Spring of Goodness." This title is prompted by two framed photos of my smiling husband that sit on my desk. I snapped the two shots when we were on our study tour of the Holy Land. The setting for the pictures was En-gedi, where the Old Testament hero David hid from King Saul and his 3000 mightiest hand-picked warriors (1 Samuel 23:29–24:2). Jim stood in the exact place for both pictures—but each has its own tale to tell!

In Picture #1, Jim is standing in front of a rushing torrent of water falling a hundred feet into a teal-blue pool. We visited this basin of refreshment on the same day we climbed Masada. Yes, this was the second dusty, dirty, dry—and, of course, steep—trek on that one single day. The trail was also very rocky. This place was a perfect hideout for David because of all its rocks and caves…and water!

After trudging up, up, up, and up, over, and around rocks and boulders, our group finally reached our destination— the life-giving waterfalls of En-gedi. En-gedi means "fountain of the wild goat" (and, believe me, you have to be a wild goat to get there!) or "spring of the kid."[1] And it was definitely a refreshing sight for sore eyes—as well as a refreshing treat for tired feet!

The small year-round spring that feeds these falls creates a cool, calming, and energizing oasis in the desert wilderness. Children splashed and played in the pool. Adults waded, relaxed, and swam. A shadow cast by the sheer rock wall and green undergrowth and trees served as a cool, welcoming embrace after a blistering hot day of physical exertion, thirst, dirt, and rocks.

We knew in advance from our trip guide that En-gedi was a favorite refuge and hiding place for David. Well, it was easy to imagine what this sanctuary meant to David. That one little spring provided everything he needed for safety and for life. It's not hard to think David may even have been looking at the rocks around the spring when he described God as "my rock and my fortress" (Psalm 31:3), "the rock that is higher than I" (Psalm 61:2).

And the second photograph? Jim stood in the very same spot, but turned his body 180 degrees. The background for this picture is the Dead Sea, a body of water so vast that it claimed the full expanse of my camera range! Forty-nine miles long, ten miles wide, and 1300 feet deep, the Dead Sea is fed by the Jordan River at the rate of six million gallons of fresh water a day.

Sounds good, doesn't it? But the Dead Sea is a salt sea and therefore virtually useless. As the saying goes, "Water, water, everywhere, but not a drop to drink!" Situated in a desert land, parched for lack of water, the Dead Sea is good for nothing. There's so much of it. And it's so blue, so inviting—yet it poisons those who drink. Truly it is a Dead Sea…and a sea of death.

A Heart of Goodness

With these two pictures in mind, let's go back to the wise mom who is teaching Proverbs 31:10-31 to her son. She's a faithful mom who lives out God's picture of true beauty. She's showing her young son one snapshot after another—one verse after another—of God's beautiful woman so he'll recognize her when he sees her.

In this picture in the photo album—this snapshot of verse 12—we are looking right into the heart of God's ideal woman. And is it ever stunning! That's because we can see that hers is a heart of goodness. How refreshing it is in our day of self-ishness—of self-centeredness and obsessing over self-esteem and self-image—to come across a woman whose heart is a selfless spring of goodness.

Now, the question for us is, How is her heart of goodness demonstrated? We already know the woman in Proverbs 31 is married and has a home and children who receive her good-ness day in and day out. But her *qualities* are what you want to focus on. So as an exercise, continue to imagine yourself striving to be more like this kind of woman now.

The presence of good—"She does him good," Proverbs 31:12 (NKJV) tells us. The woman God shows us in this verse has set a goal to shower every possible good upon others, and so should you. She lives to love others, to do them good at every opportunity, to make people's lives easier and bet-ter. Each day her prayer and the desire of her heart is to do good—to serve and help the people she encounters through-out her day. She isn't looking for any payoff. She's not after any notice or praise. She is simply following through on God's assignment to do good.

And where does all this goodness come from? How can you keep on giving God's goodness to people day after day? As a woman who belongs to God, goodness is part of what

God weaves into your character. Doing good is who you are supposed to be and what you are all about.

The absence of evil—Sometimes we learn more about something by looking at opposites, and that's what we see in this verse. "She brings him [them] good and not evil all the days of her life" (Proverbs 31:12). Our P31 lady gave out good—not evil—at every opportunity. It was a choice, and a choice you can make. You can choose to be selfish or let anger or your hurt feelings or a spirit of disapproval dictate your actions and words. Or you can choose to resist evil and instead choose to follow after God's plan to do good and not evil to the people in your life.

The influence of a lifetime—And how long did our woman from Proverbs 31 do good and refuse to do evil? "All the days of her life" (verse 12). That's the time frame God has for this lady's goodness: She was on a mission to overflow with goodness and kindness toward others "all the days of her life."

And so are you. You have this same mission assignment from God.

One way you can "bring...good" to your family and especially your parents is to "honor your father and mother" (Ephesians 6:2). And here's a thought: The only time restraint on showing respect to your parents is *your* lifetime—all the days of *your* life, not your parents' lives. In other words, there's no time limit to this honor. Just because you move out of the house to go to college or take a job or start a career or get married doesn't mean you stop honoring your parents.

Your mission to honor and respect your dad and mom

starts now—today—as you also "obey your parents in the Lord, for this is right" (Ephesians 6:1). This is the first and most important way you can do good to your parents, because it's the right thing to do.

How to Be Beautiful—Inside and Out

How can you live out a lifelong role of refreshing others?

1. Recognize the enemies of goodness—A woman of character "does...good and not evil all the days of her life." It's hard to imagine "good" and "evil" in the same verse! These two terms and their actions and intents are total opposites in behaviors. One is desirable, and the other is dreadful. Obviously the possibility of a woman failing to do good and actively doing evil must be real, or God wouldn't have to mention it. In fact, the Bible itself offers plenty of examples of women who did evil, harmful works.

Scan through this list of women who failed to be a spring of goodness for their husbands. And as you read, remember: These are the examples you do *not* want to follow!

- ❀ Eve, created to be a helper for Adam, invited him to join her in her sin (Genesis 2:18 and 3:6).

- ❀ Solomon's wives drew his heart away from God (1 Kings 11:4).

- ❀ Jezebel stirred up her husband Ahab to commit acts of abominable wickedness (1 Kings 21:25).

- ❀ Job's wife counseled him to "curse God and die" (Job 2:9).

- ❀ Rebekah willfully deceived her husband Isaac (Genesis 27).

❋ Michal despised her husband David (2 Samuel 6:16).

What could cause such chaos in a marriage? In a family? In a friendship or relationship? What is it that can cause you to choose to do evil, to choose to harm another person?

First, *a tendency to compare* yourself to others. When you compare yourself with their looks or abilities, or their popularity or any number of things, you can end up going down a dark path. A key verse to learn and mark in your Bible is 2 Corinthians 10:12, which tells you that people who "compare themselves with themselves...are not wise."

I'm sure you already know how easy it is to compare your personal life and relationships to the lives and relationships of others. Too often women of all ages can dwell on what they don't have, whether it's clothes and certain looks, or talent and a better home life. Comparisons—and expectations, dreams, and fantasies—can breed thoughts of envy and evil.

This is a far cry from God's desire for you to embrace a life mission of goodness. But you can turn your thoughts and heart around by thinking a totally different set of thoughts, like:

good life verses!

— Psalm 139:14: "I am fearfully and wonderfully made." Try acknowledging these truths!

— James 1:17: "Every good and perfect gift is from above." Your parents are one of God's gifts to you. He knows everything about them, and He's given *them* to you.

— Philippians 4:11,13: "I have learned in whatever state I am, to be content...I can do all things through Christ who strengthens me" (NKJV). Yes, you can live happily with or without whatever you have or don't have. Jesus will see you through.

Why not pause right here and right now and thank God for your family and friends and for the path He has put you on?

Another way to do good is to *make it a habit* to praise your family members. "Dad, you're the greatest!" "Mom, thanks for all you do for all of us. Is there anything I can do to help?" "Hey there, little sis! Need any help with your homework?" Let your giving heart gush at home. Then do the same for your friends—and even your enemies!

2. Get on board with the plan of God—When God gives you a mission, He also gives you everything you need to fulfill that mission. The same is true of living out God's plan for you to do good and not evil in all your relationships. God will give you all the power you need to live out His plan for you to practice goodness. So stay close to God. Read His Word. Pray. These practices will fill your heart with the goodness of God and make it an overflowing spring of goodness.

3. Plan to do good—A wise proverb says, "Do not those who plot evil go astray? But those who plan what is good find love and faithfulness" (Proverbs 14:22). I'll never forget a visiting preacher at my church sharing this verse and then pointing to the life of Adolf Hitler, the Nazi leader of the Second World War, who masterminded the murder of six million Jews. He noted that Hitler "devised evil," that he planned evil, as meticulously as a bride plans her beautiful wedding.

So, what are you planning? You can choose to plan for good—or plan for evil. But as God's beautiful woman, you are to do good. Make it your goal today and every day to plan on doing good and not evil all day long. And don't forget to follow through on your good intentions. Put your plan to work. God will help your spring of goodness to gush!

=== *An Invitation to Beauty* ===

I know Proverbs 31:12 refers to the goodness of a woman who was married. But in the context of Proverbs 31:10-31, it is part of God's instruction and description of the qualities a young single woman should possess. Remember that the young man hearing these instructions from his mother was single, and he would be seeking these virtues in an unmarried woman.

Clearly, God's goal for all of His women—young or old, married or single—is that they be a perpetual spring of goodness.

So, now, my beautiful young friend, look full into God's wonderful eyes of love and wisdom—and goodness—and choose to do good and not evil to others all the days of your life. I know you can do it, because God will help you every step of the way.

Some ABCs of Goodness

A—Always contribute spiritually. Don't discourage others about God's plans as Job's wife did (Job 2:9).

B—Bless others. Let "the law of kindness" (Proverbs 31:26 NKJV) rule your words whenever you talk about others.

C—Control your emotions, especially anger.

D—Discipline your mind and heart to think of others instead of yourself (Philippians 2:4).

E—Encourage other people's dreams. Be an encourager of their goals and ambitions.

F—Follow your parents' leadership. Eve brought sin and sorrow into the world by not following authority.

G—Give the gift of joy to those in your home. Refuse to be contentious and negative.

H—Habitually exhibit a steady, even-keeled nature. Be sure there's no Dr. Jekyll and Miss Hyde in your home!

I—Indulge in praising others. Let your mouth be a spring of goodness. "A word of encouragement does wonders" (Proverbs 12:25 TLB).

J—Join your family in activities, games, and outings. Try being a little silly at times and join in the family fun.

K—Keep up your spiritual growth. Seeking the Lord regularly is the best way to contribute goodness to your family.

L—Look not at what others have. Be content—and delighted—with God's provision for you.

M—Make prayer a part of your ministry to your family. Nothing creates a deeper spring of goodness in a heart!

N—Now try your hand at finishing this alphabet of goodness! Refer to it daily—and, of course, do it!

O—

P—

Q—

R—

S—

T—

U—

V—

W—

X—

Y—

Z—

Study Questions

Using your Bible, read through Proverbs 31:10-31. Then write out verse 12 here:

She brings him good, not harm, all the days of her life.

What do these verses teach you about doing good to all people?

Proverbs 3:27—

Do not withhold good from those to whom it's due, when it is in your power to act— when an opportunity comes to do good, take it!

Galatians 6:10—

When we have an opportunity, let us do good to all people, especially the family of believers.

Ephesians 2:10—

We are God's handiwork created in Christ to do good works which God prepared in advance for us to do.

Jot down a few acts of goodness you plan to do this week for your family members. Check here when you are finished, and then make a plan for next week. _____

Ask & do stuff for my family.
Be willing.

What was the most exciting truth or information you discovered in this chapter?

As a woman, it is my purpose to do good & desire to make people's lives easier.

How did this chapter challenge you to grow in goodness?

This challenged me to not compare myself to others.

4

A Fountain of Joy

Your Heart

"She seeks wool and flax,
and willingly works with her hands."

PROVERBS 31:13 (NKJV)

Join me for a moment or two on another walk. This one was through the streets of Old Jerusalem…and it wasn't necessarily a pleasant walk. Adventurous? Yes. Educational? Yes. Pleasant? No, as our senses were assaulted with various sights, sounds—and smells!

Crowds of people were everywhere—shoppers jostling us in their hurry, merchants and hawkers shouting and grabbing at us as we passed by their stalls. Animals used for transportation and delivery purposes made their different noises—and left various sights and smells behind! Raw meat with the layers of flies grew old and rank with the heat of the day as they hung in the meat stalls. Vegetables and fruit, too, began to droop and reek.

In the midst of this sea of humanity, large numbers of buses were emitting fumes and depositing tourists. Dump trucks were contributing their diesel fumes, and the sounds of construction work came from the renovation sites. Add to this scene the midday heat, the relentless sun, and an incredible thirst—and you may have a sense of our experience. And there was no relief in sight.

And then our guide led us through one of the many closed doors that line the streets of the Old City...right into paradise. Suddenly—in a single second—we were standing in the walled courtyard of a home with a flower garden and a small patch of lush, green grass. Blooming vines grew up the walls in the shade of several olive and palm trees. Seven pillars supported the second story of a U-shaped, three-sided structure, and their graceful arches shaded a walkway.

In the very center of this lovely scene was a fountain! Imagine—coolness and shade, and water and grass and greenery after the dust and heat of the street. Imagine—silence after the clamor of the crowds, hawkers, animals, and vehicles. Yes, it was paradise.

But I want to zero in on that fountain. In the architectural tradition of its day, the entire house, the veranda, the garden, and the walkways were built around that fountain.[1] Singing with joy, that fountain provided the only sound we heard. With its gurgles and gushes, its bubbles and busyness, that lovely fountain said, "Welcome to a place where everything is cared for and every care met!"

When I think of this fountain, I can't help thinking of you and me. We are to be like that fountain of joy in our homes. Proverbs 31 is all about being a fountain of joy—of life, of love, of ministry—for others. No matter where you live, you can be a fountain of joyful energy. You can be a joyous heart at the center of the place where you live. You can be a faithful and loyal daughter and sister who willingly and willfully does what she can to make the place where you live a place of joy.

A Willing Worker

The primary ingredient for success in any venture is hard work. You probably already have some experience with this fact. But it is especially true when it comes to running a home or any other venture like taking care of yourself, your room, your clothes, and your school responsibilities.

In the verse featured in this chapter, the wise mother in Proverbs 31 who is talking her son through a list of ideal qualities in a wife addresses the ideal *heart* attitude. She points out that God's ideal woman faces her tasks and chores and responsibilities with eagerness. She doesn't shun away from hard work. Instead "she...works with eager hands" (verse 13).

The language used to show us a willing worker indicates that a P31 woman, however old she is, is one who tackles her work diligently and cheerfully. She literally "puts her hands *joyfully* to work"[2] and makes her hands "active after the pleasure of her heart."[3]

Verse 13 shows us exactly what kind of activity this diligent woman is involved in. It is weaving, which was a major part of the work the women of her day had to do.[4] They were responsible for making the clothing for the family, and wool and flax were the two basic elements needed for weaving.

So, with great energy and enthusiasm, "she selects wool and flax." After first gathering these unrefined substances, God's beautiful woman then carries out an entire manufacturing process. She starts with raw materials and ends with finished garments. She shops, chooses, buys, processes, dyes, spins, weaves the cloth, and finally, *finally!* makes the clothing.

Sounds like a l-o-t of work, doesn't it? But don't miss the message of the verse. Our verse says she does all this—and more!—with willing hands and a joyful heart.

What's in Your Closet?

Take a look in your closet and drawers, and what do you see? Clothes, right? In different styles, for all seasons, for all sorts of occasions, and in a variety of colors.

Now take a look at our P31 lady's closet and the processes behind each garment.

Let's start with *wool*. Throughout Israel's history, much of the people's clothing has been made out of wool. The large outer garment common to the Israelites called for this heavy, warm fiber. Those willing to do the work—and God's beautiful woman was—would dye the wool as they prepared it. Then, with her keen eyes and her skillful hands, her threads turned brilliant crimson, canary yellow, Phoenician purple, and dragon's blood red (verses 21-22).

Once the wool was dyed, it was ready to be passed through her creative heart and hands. After the fabric was woven, it could be then made into clothing. Decked out in these colors, you can just imagine how spectacular her family looked against the backdrop of her sun-drenched land.[5]

And then there was *flax*. The Proverbs 31 woman also works with flax. She used the fiber of this slender herb for spinning. But first the flax had to be gathered, separated, twisted, and bleached before it could be woven into fine linen and used to make inner garments, tunics, and sleepwear.

Processing the flax involved the many demanding steps of drying, peeling, beating, combing, and finally spinning it. In fact, the more flax is beaten, the more it glistens.[6]

Ah, but our girl dives into these processes. No labor was too taxing for her. No wonder she is our model of a joyful and willing worker who "works with eager hands."

A Worker of Beauty

It's true that many women do the chores at home because they have to, they're expected to, it's their workplace. But the woman who is on display in Proverbs 31 throws herself wholeheartedly into her work not because she has to, but because she wants to. Like that fountain in the center of the garden that I visited in the Old City, she is the heart of her home. Maybe she sings, hums, or whistles while she works. ☺ Whatever the case, she delights in her work.

This woman of character lives out another verse in the Bible: "Whatever your hand finds to do, do it with all your might" (Ecclesiastes 9:10). Far from murmuring and grumbling and complaining about life's demands, she works hard, and she does it with a happy heart. She goes all out. She doesn't merely do her work. Oh no! She does it willingly and joyfully.

A part of her payoff is the pleasure she receives as she works, and when she completes the finished product. Some scholars have translated verse 13 to read that the Proverbs 31 woman works with the *pleasure* of her hands, with *willing* hands, with *merry* hands, with *inspired* hands! I like all of these thoughts and the positive—and beautiful—attitudes they reflect, and I hope you're getting the picture. Her bubbling heart and busy hands transform everything she touches into something of beauty.[8] ♡♡♡

How to Be Beautiful—Inside and Out

When I think about God's beautiful woman and the energy and joy that marks out how she does her work, I want it. I want that same kind of energy and joy when I approach my work, my projects, my tasks—and I'm hoping you want it too. Well, I've been experimenting over the years with what I now call my "attitude helpers." Besides helping me get more work done, they help me do my work with a willing heart, a happy heart. I hope these ideas do the same for you.

1. Prayer always helps—Pray for those you serve and for yourself. And pray specifically about your attitude toward your chores and your schoolwork. Because God listens and responds, prayer changes things. Your Lord can definitely turn your heart into a fountain of joy.

2. Use Scripture for a pep talk—Make a list of verses right out of God's Word that encourage you to be joyous in your work. My favorite is Psalm 118:24 (NKJV)—"This is the day which the Lord has made; [I] *will* rejoice and be glad in it." When you've got verses like this one in your heart and mind, and recite them as you work, you'll find yourself rejoicing in the Lord always, as Philippians 4:4—another great attitude helper—says!

3. Do your work "as to the Lord"—When things seem unbearable or impossible and my perspective gets warped, another encouraging verse comes to my rescue. Colossians 3:23 says, "Whatever you do, do it heartily, *as to the Lord and not to men*" (NKJV). I must remember that the *what*, the *who*, and the *why* of my work is God Himself. This reminder pours fresh new joy into my empty heart, and it will do the same for you.

4. Tackle your tasks wholeheartedly—As you face each task (yes, even your homework!), make a conscious decision to tackle it energetically and joyfully. A halfhearted attitude will produce halfhearted results.

5. Tackle your tasks energetically—Whatever chore you face, take on the challenge and "do it with all your might" (Ecclesiastes 9:10). That's how Nehemiah and the people of Israel approached the seemingly impossible task of rebuilding the walls around Jerusalem (Nehemiah 2)—they "worked with all their heart" (4:6)! And they got the job done in 52 days, an unbelievably short amount of time. They were on a mission. And so are you.

6. Tackle your tasks creatively—There is nothing worse than a boring task. Your challenge is to make it interesting. To help make it exciting, always ask yourself, "How can I do this task differently? What would make this job more fun? What can I do to make this more enjoyable?" And my favorite? "How can I beat the clock—do the work faster, finish sooner, zip through it?" (Hint: This one usually involves a timer or stopwatch.) Do whatever you can to make a game out of your work.

7. Tackle your tasks joyfully—Just as the heart of God's beautiful woman is a fountain of joy, yours can and should be too. Sometimes when I read this verse about her happy heart,

I feel jealous. I want her joy, her willingness to work, the pleasure she derives from what she views as her labors of love. I believe the key to her joy is the fact that she looks at her work with anticipation rather than dread. She sees her tasks as challenges rather than drudgery. Her positive outlook springs not merely from love for her family, but also from her joyful habit of looking at each demanding task of life and deciding to do it, to do it well, to do it as to the Lord, and to enjoy doing it!

An Invitation to Beauty

When I climbed to the top of Masada—a high rock plateau with steep cliffs—I did it one step at a time. And that's exactly how you will achieve the excellence of God's Proverbs 31 woman. She did her work with a happy heart, a joyful heart. She reaped God's forever praise by willingly doing her work one day at a time and one task at a time.

How you live each day is your "one step at a time." It's all about doing your work to the Lord and how you do it.

So what can you do today?

How will you live today?

Do you have a plan for today?

And how closely will you walk with God today?

The closer you walk with God during the next 24 hours moves you closer to being the person He wants you to be—His beautiful-on-the-inside young woman.

Study Questions

Using your Bible, read through Proverbs 31:10-31. Then
write out verse 13 here:

She selects wool and flax and
works with eager hands.

What key attitudes and actions toward work do you find
in these verses?

Nehemiah 8:10—
This day is holy to our Lord.
Do not grieve, for the joy of
the Lord is your strength.

Ecclesiastes 9:10a—
Whatever your hands find
to do, do it with all your
might. (Don't let iniquities of life keep
you from dedicated work...we work for the Lord,
not ppl."

Philippians 3:13-14—
Press on toward the goal to
win the prize.

Philippians 4:13—
I can do all things through
Christ who gives me strength.

Colossians 3:23—

Whatever I do, do it with all my ♡, as if working for the Lord, not human masters.

Check the verse you want to remember this week.

What was the most exciting truth or information you discovered in this chapter?

This was the exact message I needed to hear today. After being out of the Word a while, God still has a way of letting me know i he cares about me.

How did this chapter challenge you to develop a happy heart and a good attitude toward your work?

Because I am in college & have a terrible case of senioritis, complacency, & laziness, and I also have several things I have to get done that are due, this lesson really touched me. I can attack my work with joy rather than laziness and anger, and I am ultimately doing my work for God's glory—not mine or my professors'.

5

An Enterprising Spirit

Your Initiative

"She is like the merchant's ship;
she brings her merchandise from afar."[1]

PROVERBS 31:14

Don't you just love the Christmas season? I mean, what's not to like? Every girl loves gifts. Plus there's lots and lots of super special food. And each celebration reminds you of Christmases past. But best of all is thinking about God's greatest gift to the world—Jesus.

One Christmas, our family was invited to a special holiday open house. After the guests took turns sharing their childhood memories of Christmas, our hostess told her story as well. She described a particular custom that was observed in the European country where she grew up. On Christmas Eve, the wealthy people of the town would open their front drapes and allow others to press their faces against the windows and look inside their elaborate homes.

As a child, our friend had stood many Christmas Eves peering through exquisite panes of beveled glass at the furnishings, decorations, Christmas trees, and food in those mansions. On that one rare evening of the year, she could look through those windows and take in the beauty and riches of those who lived inside.

As you and I make our way through the 22 verses in Proverbs 31 that reveal how God's beautiful woman took care of her loved ones, I feel like God is allowing us to press our faces against the windows of this woman's home. As we peek through the windows God provides in His Word, He shows us what her eager and enterprising spirit looks like. And an added bonus is seeing how it blesses those she loves.

Profile of a Self-Starter

Over and over in Proverbs 31, in verse after verse, you can't help but notice the character qualities that shine in this woman, this God girl. Whenever I read verse 14, all I can think is, *Wow, is she ever full of energy!* I love how this verse begins: "She is *like*…" And then, as I read the entire verse, my imagination goes wild when I see that she is "like the merchant's ship."

Have you ever been sailing? There's nothing like it! Our family began sailing with friends when my daughters were two and three years old. And the sensation is thrilling. It's stimulating. It's a real high. And here in this verse, we watch as God's beautiful woman sets out on her daily errands…like a sailing vessel, like one of the merchant ships of her day.

These vessels were swift. They were aimed at a destination. And their sails were hoisted high and wide to help the ship gain as much speed as possible. They were on the move! And they were swift with a purpose—to gather merchandise for people far and wide.

The wonderful woman God is pointing out to you here in verse 14 is doing all of the above.

Here's her deal: First, she was married. That means she had people and a place—a home—to tend to, to think about, and take care of.

Next, every morning of her life she had to get out of bed and face the day. She had to be responsible. She had to be a self-starter. And she had to plan her shopping adventures, exert her energy to get out of the house and out on the streets to find the items her family needed.

And of course she was probably on the lookout for things that were unique and unusual. Maybe a rare houseplant. Or a bright beaded belt for her clothing. Or a brilliant bird's feather for her children. Maybe even a sweet treat brought from another country. Whatever she decided to buy was purchased with her family and home in mind.

Let's Go Shopping!

Just about every female I know, from three-year-olds to grandmothers, experiences an adrenaline rush and increased heart rate when these three favorite words are uttered: "Let's go shopping!" Well, our beautiful P31 woman shopped daily out of necessity. But she clearly gave her all. For instance, she scoured the marketplace for goods that would improve the quality of life under her roof. She willingly spent her time and effort to get the job done right and to meet her goal of taking care of her loved ones.

And speaking of effort, our verse says "she brings her merchandise from afar." Yes, she traveled and walked a far distance. (Note to self: Wear comfortable shoes when shopping!)

But this description also means the special items she shopped for came from around the world, from faraway and mysterious seaports. Just look at the process of getting merchandise from "afar" as you time-travel back to our lady's day!

The ships—Merchant ships have been sailing between Phoenicia (modern-day Lebanon) and Egypt since 2400 BC. These vessels stopped in every port throughout the Mediterranean Sea, where their cargo was traded for other goods. One verse in the Bible tells us the amazing fact that some of these merchant ships took as long as three years to complete their route (2 Chronicles 9:21)!

Aren't you glad you don't have to wait three years for a special item? Thank goodness for the Internet!

The supplies—The ships that pulled into the seaports were filled with unusual and exotic goods. You name it, and it was on those ships. Many of the goods were first transported by travel caravans on land, and eventually were placed on canal and riverboats that would bring their cargo to the merchant ships, which would then go to other lands. It was truly an involved and time-consuming process.

The superhighways—Our female shopper in verse 14 probably lived inland, which means that the merchandise she saw on her shopping outings had probably traveled from the nearest seaport by caravan back to the inland cities. In fact, it's likely that a steady stream of camel caravans flowed through the homeland of our beautiful woman.

The shops—At last the goods from around the world arrived in small shops of all sizes, shapes, and styles. Permanent shops opened onto a square or street, creating a sort of outdoor mall. Portable shops were also set up under awnings and tents near the city gates and in the streets.

And, whenever a camel caravan arrived from the four corners of the world, abracadabra! A market appeared instantly wherever the camels knelt. Imagine the excitement in these desert towns when basic provisions and rare and unusual items arrived by camel in the village streets!

Going on a Mission

Now look again at how our beautiful woman from Proverbs 31—*like* these merchant ships—is on a mission to bring her merchandise from afar.

Her family is the primary reason she searches far and wide. She has mouths to feed and a house to furnish and decorate. So, motivated by her heart of love, she goes the extra miles (literally!) to provide the best for those at home.

You've got family too. So try this—the next time you're out shopping with Mom or your girlfriends, think about your brothers and sisters, your mom and dad. Keep your eye out for some little something that would surprise them and make them smile. Sometimes you don't even have to spend a dollar to pick out some cool eraser, pen, stickers, or a tiny box, or a finger puppet. Even some kind of weird or tasty candy.

Creativity is also a strong factor in motivating the P31 woman. She's a creative artist! For example, because her home had no refrigeration, she shopped daily for the ingredients she needed for each day's meals. This responsibility could easily become a drag. Her daily outings could have been a dreaded chore. But no, she saw them as an adventure! Her excursions were a daily source of stimulation for her creativity in her decorating and her cooking.

Are you catching the spirit of this woman? Sure, we all have work to do. I'm sure your mom gives you a list of chores that are tailor-made just for you. You've got your room to take care of. And then there are your clothes. If you have a little brother—or sis—you probably get tapped at some point each day to babysit or watch over or entertain your sibling.

Like the example God gives us in Proverbs 31, you can turn each work chore or responsibility into a wonderful opportunity to be creative. Challenge yourself to see how much you can get done or how fast you can do your work. Put on some music and hum yourself through your jobs. Like our P31 woman, don't complain. Don't grumble. Don't sulk. Don't tell Mom exactly how you feel about what she's asking you to do. Don't wish you didn't have to do it. Just head into your work and sail through it!

How to Be Beautiful—Inside and Out

Are you wondering, *Just where is the energy for doing my responsibilities going to come from?* Here are some key ingredients for creating the kind of beauty God is showing you in Proverbs.

1. Work on a heart of love—The Bible says that without love we are nothing (1 Corinthians 13:2), and let's add that without love, we will want to do nothing!

So…*make love a priority*, starting right at home within the four walls where you and your family live. You are on assignment from God to love your parents and your brothers and sisters. Your family and the place where you live is the first place where your love should be given. Your love should—and will—make a difference in your home and family.

2. Work on your creativity—Whatever you love to do, share it. Use it to bless others. My granddaughter Katie makes paracord bracelets. At first it was a challenge, but she made a special bag out of duct tape to hold all her bracelet-making supplies. Everywhere Katie goes, you'll find her using spare minutes and time waiting in the car braiding her next exciting bracelet creation. She's gotten so good at it that she brought in quite a lot of money for her Awana group's camp fund drive. Then she made a special bracelet to give each of the girls in her cabin at camp.

3. Turn your daydreams into a reality—Spend time with people who are creating something beautiful. I don't have to tell you to study magazines. Search the Internet. Check out library books. Make it a point to stop into gift shops and bookstores. Find out how much you can discover and learn from what you see around you.

When I was on a book tour in Ireland, we visited the grounds of Glenarm Castle. I have quite a basket collection, but I had never seen a basket being made from step one. At the castle festival, I got to stand, watch, and talk with a woman who turned twigs, reeds, and bush branches into works of art. She was literally weaving her magic!

And you too can turn your dreams into reality and bless others if you're a self-starter with a heart filled with love—God's love.

An Invitation to Beauty

Can you hear it? God is calling you to be energetic and creative. To take the initiative. To be a self-starter. Look to Him first. Then take a look at your life. Who lives in your home, and how can you touch their lives with your energy? With your care? With your creativity? Put another way, how can you make their lives better? More beautiful? More pleasant?

And take a look at your heart too. Is it filled with love for others, especially your parents and siblings—however pesky and needy they may be?

The secret or key to all this love and energy is God. Loving God and wanting to do and be what He wants you to do and be will motivate you to pay any price and put forth every effort. And, when you love Him and grow more like Him, you will find yourself loving people...just like He does.

Study Questions

Using your Bible, read through Proverbs 31:10-31. Then write out verse 14 here:

She is like the merchant ships, bringing her food from afar.

In your Bible, read Proverbs 9:1-6. Describe the scene in this wise woman's house—her food, her table, her home, her work, her goals, and the results.

Parallels to the banquet Jesus describes in Luke 14:15-24. The results are a beautiful banquet table full of wholesome and healthy food and wise company.

What traits were key to her character and her homemaking?

She is wisdom, representing a woman of character.

Now read Proverbs 9:13-18. What do you observe about
this woman's house—her food, her table, her home, her
work, her goals, and the results?

She is a prostitute with
stolen food. This is representative
of the fall of Adam and Eve
and she is trying to entice
people by telling them that being
bad feels oh so good.

Why was her homemaking so different from that
described in verses 1-6? Wisdom vs folly.
As opposed to wisdom, folly
represents the wickedness that
can sometimes be enticing and
pleasurable, but these are temporary.
The satisfaction wisdom brings, however,

What was the most exciting truth or information you dis-lasts
covered in this chapter? forever.

To choose wisdom over folly.
The rewards are much greater
and the heartache isn't as
prevalent.

How did this chapter challenge you to grow in initiative,
in being a self-starter?

Like in the last chapter, I
need to approach my responsibilities
with adventure and creativity
rather than angst and
frustration.

6

A Plan for Your Day

Your Discipline

"She gets up while it is still night;
she provides food for her family
and portions for her female servants."

PROVERBS 31:15

I couldn't sleep—I was just too excited! Finally Jim and I arrived in Jerusalem after 15 hours of flight time and a stopover in London. We had checked into our hotel room inside the Old City of Jerusalem, threw on some clothes fit for exploration, and at last, began our 21-day study course in the Holy Land. We were soooo ready—if only the sun would come up!

Finally there was enough light to catch a first glimpse of Israel, Jerusalem, and the Old City, so we trudged up the stone steps that opened onto the roof of our hotel. In no way were we prepared for time travel!

That's when I saw her. A woman on a nearby rooftop was already hard at work. Her laundry was hung on a line. Her windows were swung open, allowing the morning air to cool the stone house before the day's heat set in. Her porch was swept and scrubbed. After cutting some fresh flowers that grew there in her pots, she carried them into her home along with a handful of ripe lemons picked from her rooftop citrus trees.

I knew I was watching a real-life Jewish woman bring Proverbs 31, verse 15 alive—"She gets up while it is still dark; she provides food for her family and portions for her servant girls." I was so glad I was there to see the Bible come alive. And, I have to say, this hard-working woman gave me a fresh desire to keep trying to live out the kind of disciplined life that is beautiful in God's eyes.

"Thank You, God," I whispered, "for this glimpse—here in Your land—of a woman who gets up early and gets to work making her brand-new day count for herself and others."

Let's halt our travel adventure back in time for a reality check. Take a look at yourself today. Proverbs 31:15 is about how you can take care of *your* place, whether it's your room in your parents' home or a dorm room or an apartment. The mom who is teaching her son the ABCs of what the ideal woman looks like and what she does (Proverbs 31:10-31) knows all about three daily disciplines for success in a woman's life.

#1. Up and At 'Em!

According to our verse, a woman who contributes positively to others "gets up while it is still dark." Before you moan, remember that when Proverbs 31 was written, a woman got up early—and throughout the night—for a number of reasons.

Taking care of the fire at home—Like today, light and heat were vital at home, but they didn't come easily for our Proverbs 31 girl. So the woman of the house made sure a small lamp—like a saucer filled with oil with a wick floating in it—was kept burning all night. The fire was needed to light the household fire in the morning. She was responsible to get up several times during the night to refill the saucer with oil so her lamp didn't go out.

Taking care of the fire of her heart—Our P31 girl was a girl who "feared" or loved the Lord with all her heart (see verse 30). So an early start each day gave her time to pray and spend time in God's Word.

As you think about your life, I'm guessing heat and light are not a problem for you. Just flip a few switches, right? And you've got electrical appliances, burners on the stove, and the heater running. That takes care of a lot of creature comforts.

But what about your heart? An early start of just a handful of minutes can fire up your love for God. And even a single verse in the Bible, like "I can do all this through Him who gives me strength" (Philippians 4:13) can send you out into your day armed for any and every challenge.

So how can you get up a tiny bit earlier? Try a "backward look." Take a look back on the pattern of your days. How are you doing? Any stress? Any goofs? Any things forgotten—or done badly—due to a lack of time?

I think I know the answers to these questions because I ask them every day myself! So if you are failing on any or all of the above, this is where "backward planning" saves the day. Ask yourself: "What time have I been getting up?" Whatever your answer is, it must not be early enough, or your days would go more smoothly.

Solution? Set your alarm clock or phone alarm to go off 15 minutes earlier, or maybe even 30 minutes earlier. Prepare yourself to be surprised. Prepare yourself to have a better day.

And here's a thought: If you like to journal, take a few minutes at night and summarize your day and how it went. I know that once you begin to get up even a little earlier, you will see a massive improvement. Amazingly, big things start small. Don't you agree that a few minutes is a small investment that earns big results?

#2. Is Anyone Hungry?

Read Proverbs 31:15 again, and this time pay special attention to what God's woman is doing: She "gives food to her household." Bread was the main food staple in her day, and it was baked and provided daily…meaning someone had to get up early to make and bake it.

But there was more to making bread. This lady didn't have an electric bread maker on her kitchen counter, with a timer for mixing, raising, and baking the bread. Oh, no. There could be no bread until the grain was ground. Then the dough was mixed and shaped, and finally the small pita-like flat breads were baked on hot rocks and ashes.

So what can you do about morning preparation of food at home? You can set out the cereal boxes for the family on the breakfast counter or table. You can make your lunch for school. And you can help your younger brothers and sisters make theirs too—or even make the lunches for them.

And, as you already know so well, whenever anyone prepares food in the kitchen, there's always a mess afterward! So how about cleaning up without being asked? Do it for Mom. Do it for your family. Most of all, do it as though you are serving the Lord. As Jesus Himself said, "Whatever you did for one of the least of these brothers and sisters of mine, you did for me" (Matthew 25:40).

#3. Why Not Plan for a *Great* Day?

Our verse continues, telling us she provides "a portion for her maidservants." "Portion" refers to something that is due to another person—a prescribed portion or allowance. It's assumed that God's beautiful woman gave a portion of food to her maids. After all, they were members of her household. But she also gave them work to do. She gave them instructions that outlined their daily work assignments.

You know the saying—A woman's work is never done. Well, like you, our P31 woman had work to plan and organize for herself, as well as for any others she depended on for help. I'm guessing you don't have servants to give orders to! But be sure to have a plan for your day—a plan that will make it a great day! And remember, if you don't plan your day, someone else will be happy to plan it for you—and you sure don't want that to happen!

A Pattern for Success

As one of God's beautiful young women, you can have success today, centuries later, by following this woman's pattern—she got up early. That's a simple but not always easy thing to do. Just think of the many blessings that are yours when you get up even a little earlier than those in your home or dorm.

Time alone—I hear a lot from women young and old that they just don't seem to have any time alone. Their days are filled with constant interruptions. They are always getting a call, a text, or an email. Family members are buzzing about. The TV is usually blaring. You just can't find any peace and quiet!

By now you know God's solution: Get up earlier! In the quiet calm of dawn, you can have some precious time alone.

Time with God—When you get up a little sooner, you'll have time to spend with the Lord. Time to pray about the important people and events in your day and your life. Time to mentally walk through your day and your schedule. Time to prepare for the challenges ahead.

Honestly, I can't think of anyone who gets up each morning and says, "I think I will walk out of my house or dorm with no thoughts or plans for the day. I'll just take potluck, thank you very much! Time with God? Nope, I've got this covered. I'm good."

No, smart girls look at their schedule. They even ask their parents for direction and input. And really smart girls make sure they never leave their room without checking in with God for His direction for the day. That's what time with God gives you—direction for your day. After all, no one cares more about your day than God does, because it's not your day—it's His. It's a day He wants you to live—to *really* live!

Time to plan—A handful of quiet minutes alone before the rush of the day begins also means time for planning. For what? For that next exam. For a paper that needs to be written for English class. On and on goes your list of things that need planning.

This, my friend, is what is called *time management*. One top time-management expert wrote this: "I do almost all my planning early in the morning. I...average...three and a half hours a week at it. I wake up around 5 a.m., before anyone

else in the house, and I put this quiet time into my most important activity—planning."[1]

Wow! Well, maybe one day you will reach this person's level
of responsibility or attention to detail. After all, planning is how
all good things come to pass—how books get written, how
skills at a sport are improved, how one earns a prized chair in
the orchestra. In short, planning is how dreams come true and
responsibilities are met and fulfilled head-on. So plan to plan!

How to Be Beautiful—Inside and Out

You've probably already heard too much about getting
your beauty rest—and oh, don't we love it…and need it! But
don't forget that getting God's kind of beauty by getting up a
little early is even more important. Think about the value of
the beauty of order! No one can put a price on it. So, instead
of living a life marked by the helter-skelter of things lost, forgotten, or misplaced, instead of days characterized by running behind and never getting around to it, and punctuated
by "Oops!," "Eek!," and "Oh, no!"—work on the discipline of
getting up early. Just this one thing!

And it's not as hard as you think. Read on…

First, determine a time—You probably won't start your day
two or three hours before daylight, as the P31 woman did. But
you can probably figure out what is the best time for you to
get up so you can complete your planning and preparations
for the day. Then design your ideal morning routine.

Next, get yourself to bed—You might find it possible to burn
your candle at both ends for a little while, but eventually you

will burn out from tiredness! So try moving your bedtime up an hour. Or at least get into your bed an hour earlier. You can still use that hour to write in your journal, go over your notes for tomorrow's quiz, read a chapter in your just-for-fun book… and maybe even drift off to sleep earlier than you would have if you hadn't planned to be in bed earlier.

Then say a prayer—Pray as you turn out your light. Center your final thoughts on the Lord and all you desire to accomplish for Him tomorrow with your fresh new day. Hopefully you can pray as Susanna Wesley prayed: "Lord, thank You for a meaningful day, for 'a day well spent,' for I have offered my life and this day to You as a 'living sacrifice.'"

Finally, get up!—When you hear the sound that wakes you up tomorrow, roll over, sit up, put your feet on the floor—and get up. Then go ahead and stretch and smile…and take your first step into your bright new awesome day! Live it and love it. Jesus stated, "I have come that they may have life" (John 10:10), and, as I heard one preacher put it, "That you might *really* live!"

An Invitation to Beauty

God's beautiful Proverbs 31 woman models for you the discipline of getting up early. As you comb through the 22 verses that describe her beauty, you will see this one discipline touching and bettering every area of her life.

Time spent praying and planning and preparing before the ground starts to shake gives you a master plan that works for your day and brings the beauty of order to your life.

So, as every time-management expert advises, "Up and at 'em!"

✷ Pray every morning and give God my life, dedicating the day to Him.

Study Questions

Using your Bible, read through Proverbs 31:10-31. Then
write out verse 15 here:

*She gets up while it is still night;
she provides food for her family
and portions for her female
servants.*

As you read about this woman, how do you see her
spending her day?

She is very productive!

Think about the people in her life. Who were they, and
how were they blessed by her efforts?

*Her family. They knew they
were very loved and looked
after and*

List the key people in your daily life.

— How do you benefit or help or bless them on a daily basis?

— How could you do more?

What was the most exciting truth or information you discovered in this chapter?

How did this chapter challenge you to be more disciplined?

7

There Is Profit
in All Labor

Your Vision

*"She considers a field and buys it;
Out of her earnings she plants a vineyard."*

PROVERBS 31:16

You've probably heard about the findings of "right brain—left brain" research. Supposedly one side of the brain controls your creative functions, and the other side influences what is practical.

Well, here in one verse—Proverbs 31:16—we see God's beautiful woman using both sides of her God-given brain to full advantage. She's obviously made it a point to work on developing both sides of her brain! In the creative realm, she's a visionary—a gal who's given to dreaming and imagining.[1] (Don't you love it?) She has goals, and wants to grow and develop herself to make sound decisions and be a blessing to others. She dreams of making a difference and succeeding in the variety of areas that make up her life.

But she doesn't stop there. She puts the practical part of her mind to work to make her dreams actually happen. In fact, we could say she is a businesswoman as well as a visionary. Sure, her dreams abound. But our girl is willing to do what must be done to make those dreams come true.

Triple Action

As a teen and young adult woman, no one has to explain dreams and visions to you. They seem to come with just being a girl. But you can learn a lot from the three practical concrete actions God's beautiful woman takes in verse 16 as she works to make her dreams come true. These same three steps can help you transform your own dreams into reality both now and in the future.

Step #1: Stop...and think—What does Proverbs 31:16 say? "She considers a field." Stepping back in time for a minute, imagine this scene from Bible times. The heroine in Proverbs 31 is out shopping and conducting business in the town market. While she's in the town center, she hears about a local field that's just come up for sale. As she stills her racing heart, she calmly asks a few key questions and gathers some preliminary information about the property.

Why the racing heart? Because she has a dream—a vision born out of love—that will help better her family. She's constantly been on the lookout for any chance to make her dream happen, and this field definitely looks like a golden opportunity to increase her husband's income and improve her family situation.

How does she respond to the news that this property is for sale? Does she impulsively rush to the landowner and buy the field? Does she reach into her tunic, whip out her clay credit card, and blurt, "Charge it—quick!"? No.

First, she stops and reins in her desires.

Then she puts on her business hat. Moving forward, she carefully looks at the field to determine, "Will this be a wise investment or not?" In her heart and emotionally, she wants a field. In fact, she wants it a lot! But she chooses to put her mind in control instead. She puts her heart on hold and "considers" such a purchase. Her newest goal? To learn all she can about the piece of land…so she can make a sound decision.

Next she puts her mind in high gear. It's time to get the facts. How much is the property really worth? She does her research, asks experts, and even walks the property herself. And while she's at it, she evaluates her finances—what she has, and any needs that are coming up that will require her cash.

Finally comes her personal inventory. Does she have time to take on this project and responsibility? Will anything—or anyone in her family, including herself—suffer if she takes on this new commitment?

Think about all the opportunities that come your way in just one day. From what you put on in the morning, to what you eat at breakfast, you can stop and think—consider—it. At school a friend says, "Hey, want to go to the mall after school?" Again, instead of feeling pressured or tempted or blurting out "Sure!" on impulse, you can stop and take time to consider what's best. And, if you do go shopping, at every whim and option to buy something, you can once again stop and think about it. Consider it.

Waiting and patience and wisdom are strong character qualities. Proverbs 21:5 tells us "the plans of the diligent lead to profit as surely as haste leads to poverty." So be wise! Stop and think. Take time to "consider" before you act. You will save yourself heartache, regret, painful consequences…and money!

Step #2: Make a decision and act on it—"She considers a field and buys it," verse 16 reports. Obviously, after going through Step #1—stop…and think—our girl decided that purchasing this field would be a profitable undertaking. So she bought the land.

So how exactly did she make her decision? I'm sure this wise woman, in all her weighing of the pros and cons, consulted her husband—because that would be wise. As Proverbs 31 points out, "her husband has full confidence in her," and "she brings him good, not harm" (verses 11-12).

Like her, you will want to include others in your important decisions—in this case, your parents. They have wisdom to share with you. And they are responsible for you and your decisions. Plus, asking them and checking in with them before you act builds a strong bond of trust. And if they advise you against something, you can know that it is for your good. It could even keep you out of trouble. And it can save you money.

Speaking of money, where, we wonder, does God's beautiful woman get the money to buy a field? How does she finance her vision, her field of dreams? The cash comes from her shrewd money management. It comes from her savings. Her thrift pays off in daily life as well as in this business deal.

All her efforts—her management, her work, her industry, her doing without, her saying, "No"—helps furnish the money that makes one of her dreams come true when a prize opportunity comes along. As someone has said, "Hard work is the yeast that raises the dough!"

Step #3: Fix it up—"Out of her earnings she plants a vineyard" (verse 16). Our woman of excellence not only purchases a field. She also plants a vineyard there. With her hard-earned, well-managed, carefully and faithfully saved money, she has enough revenue to buy a field and also select and plant a vineyard with the best starter plants her funds could buy.

How to Be Beautiful—Inside and Out

Let's get practical. We've talked about dreams, and how important they are, and how to make them come true. In a few words, they come true when we seek and follow God's wisdom and add our own hard work to the pursuit. So put these important how-tos to work for you to make your visions become reality.

Desire God's beauty—Ask the Lord to build in your heart a treasure chest of beautiful character qualities. Ask Him to help you build:

❀ Patience—so you will be able to wait before you act when opportunities cross your path

❀ Prudence—which is an old-fashioned word for discretion; this means that you will carefully think things over while you are waiting and making a decision

❀ Prayerfulness—to guarantee you seek God's will and wisdom while you're waiting and thinking about your dream

❀ Petition—meaning you willingly consult your parents or youth leader before making a decision

❀ Purpose—so you focus your heart in the right direction, in God's direction

❀ Perseverance—so you will hang in there and do whatever it takes to make your dreams come true

Devote yourself to God's goals—As His girl, your goals include loving Him, growing in your knowledge of Him, wanting to do what He wants you to do, and taking on more and more of His beautiful character. The pursuit of these goals will cause you to be beautiful inside and out.

Please your parents—Don't let your dreams violate your family's trust in you. How is this done? By willingly submitting your personal dreams and desires to those of your parents. By making sure you "obey your parents in the Lord, for this is right. Honor your father and mother" (Ephesians 6:1-2). By wanting God's beauty and the qualities He wants in you. By consulting your parents on the issues you face in and out of the home.

Wow, what a daughter you'll be. Your parents will be smiling inwardly as you present your cases and choices. They'll be trying to keep a straight face, thinking, *Here she goes again! She's truly amazing! Where does she get such great ideas? And where does she get her energy?! Wow, what a daughter!*

Dream away!—What is your vision of the future? If you could earn a little extra money, what would you love to do? As you think about the desires of your heart and the abilities

God has given you, what kinds of skills would you like to build? Like the woman in Proverbs 31, who was intelligent, creative, and driven—a self-starter, for sure—you can use your creativity for practical purposes. You'll love doing what you love. You'll like any money you earn. And best of all, others will be blessed.

Are crafts your passion? Why not put them on a craft table for donations for church camp? Or maybe you're great with kids and excel at babysitting. Do you like helping people? Think about walking the neighbor's dog, or feeding their cat, or washing their car.

Make your list of things you love to do. And keep adding to it. Whatever you do, please, please, please don't forget to dream! Polish your vision…and move toward it.

Do the work—The title of this chapter is from Proverbs 14:23: "In all labor there is profit" (NKJV). How do dreams become reality? The progression for God's beautiful woman went like this:

Her character (verse 10) led to
her willing heart (verse 13), which led to
her industry (verse 13), which led to
her savings (verse 11), which led to
her investments (verse 16), which led to
her prosperity (verse 25).

Behind every success story is plain ol' hard work—powered by love for others, a vision of their well-being, a dream about how to make that happen, and God's gracious blessing!

An Invitation to Beauty

Now for you, my friend with hidden talents galore! I could be writing these same beautiful truths about you. I want you to dream right now, to consider your field of dreams. Take an evening off from TV. Turn off your music. Ignore the computer. Halt or remove whatever it is that keeps you from thinking creatively, from dreaming and wondering and planning.

Now describe your dream—or ten of your dreams—and pray! Then start through this process for making your dreams come true, praying all the way through. It will take time and effort to make your dreams on paper become reality, but you can do it! Slowly but surely, there is profit in all labor. You will reap rewards and see progress as you step by step, day by day, move toward your vision. When you work hard and mix in God's wisdom, your dreams can come true. And when good dreams come true, others are blessed…and so are you.

Study Questions

Using your Bible, read through Proverbs 31:10-31. Then
write out verse 16 here:

*She considers a field and buys
it; out of her earnings, she plants
a vineyard.*

Hard work makes dreams a reality. But what happens to
those who don't work hard, according to these verses?

Proverbs 6:10-11— *A little sleep, a little
slumber, a little folding of the
hands to rest—and poverty will
come on you like a thief & scarcity like
an armed man.*

Proverbs 10:4—
*Lazy hands make for poverty,
but diligent hands bring wealth.*

Proverbs 19:15—
*Laziness brings on deep sleep,
and the shiftless go hungry.*

Name one dream or idea you would be willing to work
hard on to make it a reality.

Blogging ☺

What first step must you take?

Pray about it and think
of examples.

What was the most exciting truth or information you discovered in this chapter?

It will be a blessing to others
when I use my talents
productively.

How did this chapter challenge you to enlarge your
vision?

I cannot be lazy to
succeed in my dreams.
Hard work is key.

8

A Go-Getter Attitude

Your Work

"She sets about her work vigorously;
her arms are strong for her tasks."

PROVERBS 31:17

Like an exquisite diamond with many facets, so the 22 verses of Proverbs 31:10-31 reveal a variety of sparkling qualities. When her glittering character traits are summed up, our remarkable lady shows us two sides to her beauty: She is mentally tough, and she is physically strong. Whatever challenges life brings her way, she is prepared, equipped, and able to meet them head-on.

Here in verse 17 you get to see her attitudes (her mental toughness) and her work (her physical strength). Let's start with her mental strength, because without mental toughness, you will never get around to doing the actual physical work.

Preparation for Work

How does God's beautiful woman get her work done? What is the key to her success in all that she tackles? And what does she have to show and tell us about becoming a go-getter?

91

First, Proverbs 31, verse 17, tells us, "She sets about her work vigorously." Another translation gives us the cultural picture of what's going on. It reads, "She girds herself with strength" (NKJV). These words, carefully chosen by the female teacher, instructed her son to pay special attention to a young woman's attitude toward work. When it was time for him to marry, a potential bride's attitude toward work was vital.

Three thousand years ago when Proverbs was written, women (and men too) wore garments that flowed from their shoulders to the ground. That meant they had to first gather up their dress and secure it with a girdle-like belt so they could get their physical work done. Once they had "girded their loins," they had the physical freedom of unlimited movement they needed for doing heavy labor. This girding of the gown preceded their physical work.

But this girding action was also a psychological trigger for a person's attitude. I'm sure you've put on an apron once or twice. You probably also have some work clothes and your exercise clothes, which serve as a motivator for work—or a workout—even while you're putting them on. It's like rolling up your sleeves as you get ready to go into action—to get to work.

Well, the action of gathering one's dress was key to preparing to take action. This preparation sparked a "let's go" attitude toward whatever task was in front of them. One of my favorite Bible translations says, "She girds herself to work."[1]

The next secret we uncover about her go-getter attitude toward her work is "she girds herself with strength." I don't know anything about the original Hebrew language in which the Old Testament was written, but my husband does. And he explained to me that the emphasis on this woman's physical strength and endurance shines the spotlight on her unwavering commitment to work and her ability to work hard.

And not only is she a go-getter, but she's a self-starter. It's clear that a part of her strength comes from her choice to engage in hard work—she girds herself. The girdle is a symbol of the mental and physical strength she wears as she enters the arena of her labor.

When all is said, the P31 woman's girding of herself with strength reveals that she is both motivated to do her work and prepared for the activity. This phrase could also be translated, "She dressed herself in strength!"[2]

Finally, we see that "her arms are strong for her tasks," meaning she is ready and able to work. She has prepared herself both physically as well as mentally for the effort any task requires. As one translation exclaims, "How briskly she girds herself to the task [there's her mental attitude], how tireless are her arms [and here's her physical strength]!"[3]

A Personal Formula for Work

If I were paraphrasing Proverbs 31:17 for today, I would say, "When it comes to work, the woman who is beautiful in God's eyes is ready, willing, and able!" As I've thought about this quality in God's beautiful woman, I've decided that her mental attitude is the key to the large amount of work she accomplishes, and that attitude reveals the following four qualities of the heart.

Commitment—Work is a matter of the heart, and where there is no heart commitment, very little (if any) work gets done. I know in my early homemaking days I had to make a commitment to step into the homemaking arena. I loved reading, brooding, and watching TV. But one evening I heard a Christian woman I admire say, "I don't do anything sedentary!" After I double-checked the definition of *sedentary* (meaning "inactive life" and "tending to sit down a lot"), I thought about that statement for days. In fact, I still think about it—and her— every day. I finally made a pledge to be more active, to get moving...and keep moving, to always be doing something. After all, as we've already learned, "all hard work brings a profit" (Proverbs 14:23)!

Willingness—Our willingness to do the job—whatever it is—plays a large role in how easily and quickly we accomplish our work and how much we get done. Sure, we can have a heart commitment to do the work, but we must also be willing to actually do it!

As one of God's women—a woman of character—we've enlisted in God's army, so to speak. We've signed on. We've volunteered. So now we have to be mentally ready and willing to do or give whatever is necessary to answer the call to duty!

Motivation—For me, motivation is key to the work I do because motivation is the "why" of anything I do. I'm constantly thinking and praying about what I want for my life, my family, and my home. And I keep on praying because of what I want to contribute to my church, to God's people, and to others.

As I'm thinking about you, I'm imagining this is what you want as well. So, if you want these things badly enough, then you will be motivated to do the work that's required to make it happen (Lord willing!). Goals like these that make a difference in you and in others provide motivation for a lifetime. And that motivation gives you strength of mind—a go-getter attitude—as you tackle the work involved.

Discipline—Ouch! For me, this is the one that hurts. Up to this point, everything has been dreams, desires, goals, and talk! But, as the second half of Proverbs 14:23 so rightly states, idle chatter or "mere talk leads only to poverty." Discipline is necessary for turning talk into action and reaching goals.

And this discipline is all a matter of the mind! We fight the battle to get any kind of work done in the mind. That's where we make our choices. That's where we decide how to spend our time and energy. That, my fellow pursuer of beauty, is why mental toughness is basic to work. When you are mentally tough, you will win the battle over laziness, procrastination, disorganization, and other enemies of productivity.

How to Be Beautiful—Inside and Out

Beauty begins on the inside, and a few key internal exercises that will help you work up a stronger go-getter attitude. You'll even notice an eagerness about your work.

1. Know God's will for your life—If you aren't sure what God's will for you is, you're seeing it expressed right here in Proverbs 31. This passage is His portrait of a godly woman. So study these 22 verses of the Bible and learn them by heart. Put their messages in your own words—and own them. Love them. Tackle them. Be committed to them. Then watch to see how God transforms your beauty from the inside out.

2. Stay in God's Word—Exactly where will the strength and

motivation and desire to be what God wants you to be come from? From God's Word. From the Holy Spirit using the Scriptures to energize your heart, mind, and strength. In verse 30 we discover that God's beautiful woman loved and feared the Lord. Her goals were those communicated in His Word, and her strength was empowered by His Word. The same is true for you, O beautiful one!

3. Know the why—It's vital to know *why* you are doing what you do. Why? Because the *why* will motivate the work. Some unknown teacher put it this way: "The secret of discipline is motivation. When a man [or woman] is sufficiently motivated, discipline will take care of itself."

And it's true. You can know what needs to be done. And you can possess all the necessary skills to get it done. But until there is motivation, which comes from an understanding of *why* something is extremely important, the job probably won't get done.

4. Pray to be a go-getter—When you turn off your light at night, pray about the work you know is coming tomorrow. Ask God to help you greet the day with an eager attitude and keep you positive all day long. Then, when the alarm goes off in the morning, thank God for another day, and go get 'em!

5. Make a schedule—A daily schedule helps you plan your work. It will remind you of what's coming and where you're going. With a schedule you'll be able to anticipate the pace each project requires and complete your many tasks right on time.

6. Develop a routine—The more work you are able to fit into a daily routine, the better. Think about those things you do every day—spending time with the Lord, getting dressed, riding the bus or meeting the car pool, doing homework, practicing for your sport. Your goal is to be able to say, "This is when I always…do this." Because you will get so used to your routine, you'll have fewer decisions to make, less thinking to do, less indecision, less temptation to skip out, not to mention less time wasted as you waffle around about what to do next. And you will perform so many tasks by rote that your mind will be free to talk to God throughout the day, plan what's important to you, and dream your beautiful dreams.

7. Tackle the worst first—Do you find yourself living your days under a cloud of dread just because there's some challenging or unpleasant task you need to take care of? Unload that burden by doing that task first! Once the monumental thing is out of the way, the rest of your day will be smooth sailing. Clearing the major hurdle in your day first thing will give you a rush of fresh energy for what's left.

8. See how fast you can work—Make doing your chores and your work a game. How long do you think a job will take? Then try to beat the clock. Continue to better your times, to make that task take less time. And what's your reward? Having more time to spend on fun things, on pursuing your own creative abilities and hobbies.

An Invitation to Beauty

I know lots of people who don't even like to *think* about being a go-getter. But just one read through Proverbs 31:10-31 proves that God wants you to make it to becoming like this beautiful woman. He wants you to make it to the heights of her beauty and glory. And so do I.

As I read again the two paragraphs in the section on "Motivation" (please read it again too), I realized I was listing all the things I want for my life. But, my friend, believe me when I say I want them for you too! Why? Because God wants both of us—and all His women—to accomplish His will, to do the work He has given us, the work that makes other people's lives better. Now *that's* true beauty!

Study Questions

Using your Bible, read through Proverbs 31:10-31. Then write out verse 17 here:

She sets about her work vigorously; her arms are strong for her tasks.

In a few words, describe your usual attitude and actions when you have to get up each day. What thoughts are running through your head? (My favorite is, "Oh no, not another day!" Most days, I also add, "I have so much to do I'll never get it all done. Ugh!")

I'm usually just still really sleepy.

— How does Psalm 118:24 help you with a go-getter attitude?

The Lord has done it this very day; let us rejoice today and be glad.

Jesus has already "been there, done that." and he will be with us as we tackle the day.

— What does Philippians 2:14 say you are *not* to do?
How do you think this would help you when you
first wake up? When you have to do your homework? When you have to do your work chores at
home? We are to "do everything
without grumbling or arguing."
There is no use in complaining
if a job needs to get done.

One Bible translation of verse 17 says, "She gets ready to
work hard" (NIrV). List three ways you already get ready
to work hard each day.

—

—

—

Now list three things you could add to this list that would help you get ready to work hard each day.

— Decide my outfit & hair the night before. (and have room & bathroom already clean)

— Go to bed earlier (to rise earlier)

— Have a "to do" plan set for the next.

What's keeping you from adding these three helps to your daily routine? Make a note and then…just do it.

I just need to do it.

What was the most exciting truth or information you discovered in this chapter?

It is God's will for me to be a Proverbs 31 woman & all that entails.

How did this chapter challenge you to improve your attitude toward your work?

Not just say I will actually have a plan of action, but to actually make it happen.

9

A Taste of Success

Your Confidence

*"She sees that her trading is profitable,
and her lamp does not go out at night."*

PROVERBS 31:18

What a woman! God's P31 lady does all things well. She's willing to work—and work hard. She has earned and saved money from her labor and her shrewd bargaining. There's no way to miss the obvious: This woman's high standards cause her to see success.

And what's next? Why, starting up her own little business! What I call her "Proverbs 31 Project." As our verse says, "She perceives that her merchandise is good, and her lamp does not go out by night" (NKJV).

Excellence in All Things

Hmmm. How did this woman's money-making project begin? How did it come to be? Here in verse 18 we latch onto a formula for success—in a word, it's excellence. What kind of excellence?

Great taste—Our gal "sees" that her merchandise and trading is good. For a little background information, it helps to know that the word translated "sees" is the same Hebrew word that is translated "taste" in Psalm 34:8—"taste and see that the LORD is good." So we learn that God's beautiful woman tastes and sees that her merchandise is good. She has gained a little stream of income.

How? By doing something she loves.

The process went like this: She had a dream—to better her family and to better their financial condition. So, by trial she tries first one thing, then another. She tests her ideas and learns new skills. And voila! She finds that her work is good.

By taking risks, trying out new ideas and methods, she discovers that what she's producing is good. This gives her confidence about her work.

Great goods—What exactly were the items or products she learned were so good? Well, we already know she purchased a field and planted it with crops and vines (verse 16). From her efforts she realized a profit from a dream fueled by her hard work.

Our heroine also sells her weaving. She processed wool and flax to create her yarn, created a pattern, and wove her yarn into exquisite and colorful works. Knowing that her woven clothing was good (she must have gotten a lot of compliments!), she confidently created her goods and sold them to others.

Great results—The merchandise our Proverbs princess creates and sells is "good." It's excellent. Put another way, very practically, her merchandise is profitable—and it's profitable because it's good.

Like everything else our lady did, what she produced was excellent. She gave her all. She would never put her name on something cheap or thrown together. Oh no. Others could do that...but not her. Her standard of excellence means that the work she does is top quality. And, because what she produced was so good, it brought a good price.

Great pursuit—Success fuels this woman's efforts, and we learn that "her lamp does not go out by night." With increased confidence, good results, and a profit, she works late into the night. She's motivated. She loves what she's doing. And she's on a roll. This spurs her on to work a little longer in the evenings. You know the scene—she burns a little midnight oil in that lamp of hers.

I'm sure you've stayed up late a lot of nights. Me too. There are some really good reasons for staying up—like studying for an exam or finishing homework. But there are also many less noble reasons for late-night activities. There's always TV to watch, or music to enjoy, or finishing up a real page-turner. There's talking late on the phone. Or doing your Facebook thing. Or quietly texting or surfing the Internet.

Well, the woman we're learning from in this book—the woman who is God's role model for us and all women—shows us a better way. She's got a lesson for us: If you're going to stay up late, do it for something worthwhile. Make it for a great pursuit.

What dreams or desires drive you to want to stay up late to pursue them? I know girls and women who stay up a little later than usual to work on a painting, or to sew, or to perfect a skill like jewelry-making, or to write the book of their dreams. What are your dreams, your passions?

A Pause

This seems like a good time to pause and check out this P31 lady.

— Loyal? Check.

— Busy? Check.

— Early riser? Check.

— Hard worker? Check.

— Industrious? Check.

— Creative? Check.

Do you realize that there is not one single quality or checkmark in this list for this woman that cannot be true of you too? As a young woman, a teen, a young adult, you can possess all the character qualities this woman had going for her.

With a checklist of so many solid top-notch attributes going for her, we shouldn't be surprised that her little business venture is successful. After all, she doesn't avoid hard work—and, with God's blessing, what she produces is good and profitable. She is successful in her endeavors. And she's doing something she enjoys, something that allows her to be as creative as she wants. Life is good.

How to Be Beautiful—Inside and Out

Confidence is a powerful quality. And possessing dreams and goals and pursuing them is a sure confidence builder. As an unknown "girl" tweet advises, "Never underestimate the power of a girl who knows what she wants."

To discover your areas of expertise—the areas where you excel, focus on your character. Stay busy. Be diligent. And then:

1. Listen to others—Are you getting compliments for something you do? We usually take our gifts and abilities for granted. We say, "Oh, everyone can do this. It's so easy!" and we fail to notice that no one else is doing it. That no one else is doing it with the same excellence, flair, or boldness. Sometimes we may even say, "Oh, that's not so great! Others do a better job," when we should be thanking God for the talents He's given us and trying to use those abilities in a broader way.

When someone gives you a compliment, say, "Thank you. I love doing this." Then file it away to draw on later. And, as always, remember to say, "Thank You, Lord, for giving me this ability."

2. Make yourself move on—Oh dear! Did you goof? Did the recipe fail, the paints run? Did you drop a stitch in the stocking you were knitting for a gift? Did you draw a blank when you were trying to find the right words for your writing (I can relate!) or the right notes for your music composition?

Whenever these everyday things happen, determine to move forward. Overcome these experiences by taking a page out of inventor Thomas Edison's book. This man failed thousands—yes, thousands!—of times before he invented the light bulb. His advice? "Don't call it a mistake. Call it an education!"[1]

Move on. Keep on keeping on!

3. Develop your skills—To be successful in any endeavor requires that you continue to develop your skills and techniques. My daughter Courtney had a wonderful ability and the desire to do more in the kitchen. Stepping out on her dream, she enrolled in a culinary school to develop her cooking skills.

She has "tasted" enough success to count on herself when it comes to anything in the area of food.

My daughter Katherine also actively builds her confidence. She goes to school every evening on the Internet, researching special recipes, fun table settings, and unique centerpieces and decorations for each season and celebration. She's an artistic homemaker and decorator par excellence!

Whatever it takes to develop your skills, commit yourself to it. Save for it. Get Mom and Dad's approval and support. And spend time with others who enjoy the same interests and activities. You'll not only develop skills but confidence as well.

4. Guard your time—It's true that every minute wasted is lost forever. So make it a point to "redeem" or buy back time from less-important activities so you can spend that time on your personal creative efforts. The Bible tells us we are to be "redeeming" (NKJV) time and to "make the most of every opportunity"—of every minute (Colossians 4:5).

How can you redeem or buy back time? You could watch a little less TV. You could skip a few shopping outings. You could turn off your phone, or at least mute it, for an hour— even half an hour. You could set a timer so you spend less time online or on social media.

But all of the time you spend being creative, perfecting your skills, and growing your abilities is off the scale when it comes to the satisfaction you will enjoy from achieving your potential day by day.

5. Take risks—Be creative. Try new things. Express yourself. Take on my friend Julie's attitude toward her flower arranging—"Be bold!" in whatever enterprise you are exploring.

6. Do your best—"Whatever your hand finds to do, do it with your might." That's the instruction of Ecclesiastes 9:10, and that's what the woman pictured in Proverbs 31 did. She worked with all her might and all her heart. In everything she did, her goal was to do it with excellence. And the result? Her "merchandise," her products, her results were good!

7. Do your projects unto the Lord—In the Old Testament, we are told to "commit to the LORD whatever you do" (Proverbs 16:3). In the New Testament, Colossians 3:23 echoes this advice: "Whatever you do, do it heartily, as to the Lord and not to men" (NKJV). The Lord is the reason for your work. He is your Boss. And His glory is your goal. Always, and in all things.

8. Know that what you're doing is important—You need to be convinced that your efforts are important. And usually the hardest person to convince about the value of your efforts is you! Don't forget what you've learned from Proverbs 16:18 in this chapter. You can be confident in God. And you can be confident in your God-given talents and abilities.

=== *An Invitation to Beauty* ===

Are you encouraged? Oh, I hope so! That's been my goal and my prayer for you. I'm hoping you want to follow in the P31 woman's footsteps and have the confidence to take these steps forward:

— Pour your greatest energy and efforts into your existing responsibilities—your family, your home, and your schoolwork.

— Develop solid character by learning what God wants you to be and do. Then be that person— a young woman after God's own heart, a woman who will do His will.

— Ask God for His guidance in discovering the areas you excel in. Then schedule in time to experiment and develop your skills and abilities. Count on this truth: "Delight in the LORD, and he will give you the desires of your heart" (Psalm 37:4).

— Prepare yourself to taste success!

Using your Bible, read through Proverbs 31:10-31. Then write out verse 18 here:

As you read your Bible each day and in the years to come, you'll discover a multitude of reasons you can have confidence. What resources for confidence do you find in these verses?

Ecclesiastes 9:10—

Philippians 1:6—

Philippians 3:13-14—

Philippians 4:13—

Place a check mark by the verse you want to remember this week. Then write it out here.

What was the most exciting truth or information you discovered in this chapter?

How did this chapter challenge you to grow in confidence?

10

A Little Night Work

Your Diligence

*"In her hand she holds the distaff
and grasps the spindle with her fingers."*

PROVERBS 31:19

*I*t happens every day. The sun that lights and warms the world, that energizes our life and our work, starts to sink. For many it's a welcomed signal to tired minds and bodies that another day is winding down. It's almost over. It's almost time for bed.

You know the drill: Soon there will be dinner, the sounds of clean-up in the kitchen, showers to take, teeth to brush, homework to finish, maybe a little bit of family TV time. Yes, soon it will finally be time to call it a day and go to bed.

Just about every day is a full one, isn't it? Filled to overflowing with people, challenges, commitments, responsibilities, work, creativity. And…ooooh, it's going to feel so good to finally stretch out in your favorite place of all—your bed! Rest, sweet rest! It's just around the corner.

But wait just one minute. We are learning a key lesson from

our Proverbs 31 gal. Sure, she works hard. And yes, she gets tired. But she also goes an extra mile or two after the house quiets down.

What does she do? Far from being done for the day, she does a little night work before going to bed.

Behind the Scenes

It's true that work, work, and more work lies behind every success. Clearly, the little lady from Proverbs 31 is a woman of diligence—ever persevering, continually industrious, and constantly busy. We already know she gets up early to start her work. And we know she's active all day. And now we discover that she continues to work at the end of her day too. She puts her evenings to good use.

We also know she trades off a little beauty rest for a little night work. As verse 18 says, "She sees that her trading is profitable, and her lamp does not go out at night." But what in the world does she *do* in the evening?

Verse 19 gives us a clue about one activity: She stretches out her hands to the distaff, and her hand holds the spindle. When evening arrives, she merely shifts her activities from outside in her fields to inside her home, where she works by lamplight. In her day it was perfectly natural and okay to turn in when night fell. But not our heroine. She stays up to work… just a little longer.

She continues her busyness. She works with a distaff and a spindle. These ancient objects were tools of the cloth-making trade, used for spinning wool. In a woman's hands, the distaff and the spindle transformed processed wool and flax into yarn and thread.

We learned from verse 13 that this amazing woman uses her energy to bring in, dress, clean, and untangle her wool and flax. And now, at night, as her body slows down, she sits and spins, perfecting her wool and flax for her weavings. The work may have been monotonous, but it had to be completed before she could begin weaving her creative designs.

This kind of behind-the-scenes preparation is necessary before any great work can be accomplished. For instance, before there can be a painting, the canvas must be stretched and mounted. Before a dress can be sewn, the pattern must be cut out. Before an opera can be sung, the scales must be practiced. Before a book can be written, the research must be done. Before a wall can be painted, the windows and baseboards must be masked. Before a meal can be cooked, the ingredients must be cleaned, chopped, and measured.

Most behind-the-scenes work may be mundane, routine, unglamorous, dull, unchallenging, maybe even a no-brainer. In a word, bor-ring! But preparation is fundamental to creating anything beautiful or useful.

God's beautiful woman willingly, cheerfully, heartily, and gladly (verse 13) spends her evenings doing the tedious, unexciting—but very necessary—preparatory tasks, out of which her great works of art are born.

How to Be Beautiful—Inside and Out

When I first began doing work at night rather than plopping down in front of the TV with a bowl of Cheetos and a soda, I struggled. But I'd made a commitment to use a part of my evenings to help my family and ministry. I really wanted to develop self-discipline in my new nighttime challenge.

Over time and by repetition, I gradually learned to use my evenings in more useful and creative ways. In fact, I do a lot of writing, editing, and lesson preparation at night. Now I value—and use—my evenings that were wasted for so many years. I view my nighttime hours as being like icing on a cake. Oh, the day was great, but that little bit of extra time in the evenings just makes my day.

If you're already following the example of our P31 gal, it's possible that before dinnertime, you've already finished most of your schoolwork. So now it's time for the fun to begin—your evenings become your time to shine!

As one time-management expert advises about two pockets of often-wasted hours, make your *evenings* and *weekends* count![1]

1. Evaluate your evenings—I recently heard the highest-paid sports agent in the world talk about a skill he practices every day. Speaking on the importance of time, he stated that he plans his day (every single one of them—even his weekends) in 20-minute increments. Do you know how you spend every 20 minutes of your evenings? Answering this question is definitely an eye-opening exercise!

2. Plan your evenings—One Sunday morning at church I walked right past a friend of mine. Thankfully she grabbed my arm as I went by so she could share a wonderful thing that had happened to her—she had lost 40 pounds! (That's why I walked past her—I didn't even recognize her!) When I asked her how she had done it, she told me that she had decided to exercise every night after she got home from work. Her goal for the new year had been to incorporate that one activity into her life, specifically her evenings. In other words, she planned her evenings—and she's definitely enjoying the payoff!

Believe me, it's a good thing to plan your evening early in the day. Why? Because by the time it rolls around, you'll probably be too tired to put out the mental energy it takes to even think about doing something useful! Try keeping a list of meaningful activities you can do at night. For example, you could wash and dry a load of your clothes, fold them, and put them away. You could do your nails. Thumb through your magazines. Clean out a drawer or two. Organize your craft materials. And, of course, work on your crafts!

One loud message of Proverbs 31:19 is this: Save your daylight hours—your prime energy time—for the work that demands the most from you physically and mentally. Then, when the day fades away—and your energy with it, instead of zoning out, kicking back, and plopping down, follow the example of our diligent woman. Simply change your activities.

Here's something to think about: Proverbs 10:4 tells us the person who is lazy and negligent becomes poor, "but diligent hands bring wealth." In other words, the lazy person reaps nothing, but those who are diligent succeed. They enjoy the fruit of their labors. So plan for diligence—even in the evening.

3. Prepare for your evenings—I hope you'll make your list of nighttime activities you can do. And I hope you'll plan your days as well as your nights. So before the sun goes down and you get too tired, set out the supplies you'll need for your little bit of night work. If the family is going to watch TV, set up your work on a table or coffee table. Sketch pads? Check. Craft items? Check. Art supplies? Check. Laptop? Check. Pile of magazines? Check. Manicure kit? Check.

4. Use your evenings!—It's great to evaluate, plan, and prepare, but ultimately you must use your evenings. And that calls for effort. For action. Do you remember that, in our verse, Ms. P31 "grasps the spindle with her fingers"? Well, what do your hands reach for at night? A snack? A favorite video? Your pillow? The phone? The remote control? This chapter is about diligence. And it's a call to you to make your evenings productive.

5. Use your mind in the evenings—Even if you're doing dull, routine work, your mind can be active. With a little prompting, creative sparks can fly while your hands are busy. As God's beautiful woman sat spinning her raw materials, she probably imagined what she could make with the yarn and linen, maybe even pausing to sketch her ideas. Designing in her head while her body rested and her hands sailed, she created her unique garments, deciding which ornaments would work best with the fabric, what kind of design to embroider across the yoke. On and on her mind spun. Whatever your no-brainer task is, assign your brain a creative task. Or choose a fun or serious subject to think about. Or pray for others, or for God's guidance on a decision. Or train yourself to dream!

An Invitation to Beauty

Speaking of dreaming, please don't forget to dream. To get your mind humming, name something you love to do—something personal, a passion you carry in your heart. That's a dream, my friend. Don't negate it, make fun of it, discount it, or write it off. And don't lose it! Instead, write it down in you prayer notebook or journal. And date it. Your dream or great idea is extremely important because it was borne out of your heart—the unique heart God has given you.

Now you have something you're excited about—something to pursue with a little night work.

Study Questions

Using your Bible, read through Proverbs 31:10-31. Then write out verse 19 here:

Think for a minute about your days. What kinds of routine, mundane, unexciting, maybe even boring tasks or chores have you been putting off? Is it organizing your drawers? Cleaning out your closet? Folding your laundry? Start a list here.

Now check your attitude toward these no-brainer activities. What is it that keeps you from tackling them in your spare minutes?

Read Proverbs 31, verse 13. What was this woman's attitude toward her work?

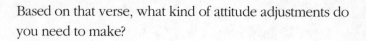

Based on that verse, what kind of attitude adjustments do you need to make?

Make another list of first steps you will take to upgrade your attitude and carry out the activities you've been putting off.

How could these verses help you?

Galatians 5:22-23—

Philippians 4:8—

You have some control over how you use your time. What do these verses say about the use of your time?

Proverbs 10:4—

Proverbs 31:27—

With your calendar or schedule in hand, notice your free time—the time that is all yours. Then schedule a few "appointments" for you to dive into your neglected projects. See what you can get done when you make a real effort…with a genuinely sweet attitude.

What was the most exciting truth or information you dis-covered in this chapter?

How did this chapter challenge you to be more diligent?

11

A Helping Hand

Your Mercy

"She extends her hand to the poor,
yes, she reaches out her hands to the needy."

PROVERBS 31:20 (NKJV)

God's beautiful woman is impressive, isn't she? My, my, she abounds in tough, strong character qualities! She's diligent. She's a hard worker. She's a whirlwind of industry. She gets up early and stays up late.

But aren't you encouraged to see that her mercy is the next item on the list of her outstanding qualities? Truly beautiful in God's eyes, the Proverbs 31 woman loves to use her resources to benefit those in her community who are in need. As God reports, "she extends her hand to the poor, yes, she reaches out her hands to the needy" (Proverbs 31:20).

Sure, she's super busy with her family and household. But she's not so busy that she forgets the needs of others. She is ever ready to bestow the soft grace of mercy to the unfortunate. Without this tender mercy, her industry and activity could make her harsh and hurried. Why, she'd be too driven and too busy to care.

Her Hand

Over the last 10 chapters, you and I have been wowed by this P31 woman's strong, energetic body. But here in verse 20 God focuses our attention specifically on her hands—and her heart.

The first part of this verse reads, "She extends her hand to the poor" (NKJV). The image of the single extended hand speaks of this lady's generous, giving nature. For instance, if money is needed, she reaches her hand into her purse and shares her wealth. If bread is lacking, she offers a homemade loaf.

And, if warm clothes are missing, God's merciful and generous woman provides one of her own handmade woolen coats (verse 21), the result of months and months and nights and nights of personal labor. In her day, a woolen garment could cost over two months' wages![1]

When it is in her power to do it, the Proverbs 31 woman extends her hand with whatever item is needed. What an example she is—a woman who lends a helping hand at every opportunity.

Her Hands

Verse 20 continues: "She reaches out her hands to the needy" (NKJV). It's obvious this woman possesses true, godly inner beauty. But her generosity doesn't end with the mere giving of things. The plural word "hands" signifies activities that require two hands.

Nursing the sick, for instance, requires two hands. So does caring for babies, young children, the elderly, and the sick. This P31 woman uses her hands for ministry. She's not afraid to roll up her sleeves and touch those who are suffering.

Whatever the need, she holds out her hands—her literal, open, upturned palms—to offer any assistance, help, or physical aid.

Her Heart

It's good to see God's beautiful woman giving, but, as the wise mother who's giving out this information points out to her boy (and to us), this woman's heart is involved. The verb "reaches out" suggests that her giving stretches as far as her means will allow.[2] Our natural fleshly nature is primarily selfish. But this kind of selfless, merciful stretching requires a heart—a generous heart of love and compassion, a heart after God.

What an example! This woman—our supreme example—gives to the poor and needy with her hand, her hands, and her whole heart. You won't find her folding her beautiful hands for selfish moments of relaxation, while others suffer, or using them to clutch her profits and hang on to her money, while others are in need, or keeping them frantically busy in order to gain even more wealth.

No, a magnificent part of her beauty is her desire to help those who are down and out. She extends her outstretched hands to those around her who are in need. She is aware of these people, sympathetic to their needs, and ready to help. Her full heart and full wallet overflow to bless others.

Instead of drawing a tight circle around herself and her family and shutting others out, she follows her heart. She opens the circle. And she takes them in. Her circle of love includes all who need her help.

Her Heart for God

When I speak to an audience, I usually allow some time for questions and answers. For years now, I've kept one particular handwritten "question" from one of my sessions. It reads, "From your study of Proverbs 31, please comment on the fact that no reference is made to the woman's involvement in 'ministry' kinds of activities."

That's an interesting inquiry, isn't it?

Well, I have to tell you that, as I look at God's beautiful woman, I definitely see that one of her ministries is taking care of the poor and the needy. You can't miss it in verse 20.

We know that her giving is generated from her heart. More specifically, it's fueled by her heart for God, her heart's desire to obey God's Word. Verse 30 tells us she's a woman who fears the Lord. In other words, she desires above all else to walk in obedience to God. That's what a woman after God's own heart is—and does: She seeks to fulfill all God's will (see Acts 13:22).

As we continue to learn what is beautiful in God's eyes, we see that caring for the poor and needy is one of His primary concerns. This beautiful, God-fearing woman knows that fact because she knows God's law and takes His commands seriously. So consider this: Perhaps the great blessing upon her personally is because of her generosity to the poor and needy. Perhaps she is wealthy not because she is a hard worker, a capable manager, or a smart businesswoman, but because God blesses her generosity. After all, God's people are God's way of caring for the poor and needy, and He in turn blesses those who care for them.

How to Be Beautiful—Inside and Out

Once you decide to work on being more generous, you'll have no trouble finding opportunities to be merciful and offer help to the poor and needy. And just to get you going down this path, try these ideas for starters.

1. Begin at home—Oh, wow. Do you realize that each sunrise presents you with chance after chance to show mercy to others—right under your own roof? If you're living at home, your parents and your brothers and sisters (even the pesky ones) are first in line for your mercy and assistance. After all, what you are at home is what you are! So be merciful, considerate, helpful, thoughtful, and generous.

2. Give to your church—Most churches minister to the homeless and needy. So through your giving you are indirectly lending a helping hand to the poor. Also, some of what you give to your church is probably used to support missionaries. When you give or tithe at church, you are extending your hand and hands in multiple directions—even around the world.

Make it a point whenever you get your allowance, or some birthday money, or some cash from a babysitting or dog walking job, to give some of it the next time you're at church.

3. Keep your ear to the ground—Take time to notice people around you who are in need. To help people, you first need to know about those who are suffering or going without. So keep your ear to the ground. Sign up to be on your church's prayer list. Don't let opportunities to do good to someone pass you by.

And just a thought—be sure you check with your parents about your plans to give money or assistance to someone or to an organization. Let them know how much and who will be the recipients of your giving. They can provide their wisdom and guidance, and they just might want to join you in your efforts.

4. *Support a group or person*—Right now I'm studying the women who followed Jesus and supported Him financially (Luke 8:2-3). Talk about supporting a worthy group or organization! Imagine being honored to contribute to Jesus and His disciples. But these women set a dazzling example for you and me. Imagine following in their steps and encouraging individuals and organizations through your financial gifts. You can contribute directly to a mission organization or support a missionary family you know.

A few dollars a month from you can support a needy child through a worthy organization. These same dollars can provide water to people who are dying of thirst in other parts of the world. Even one of your dollars is powerful when its channeled in the right direction.

Maybe you can't go into all the world and share the gospel, but your money can as you invest in causes, missions, and missionaries. Oh, and don't forget—talk it over with your parents first.

5. *Live out love*—When asked what love looks like, the early church father Augustine replied,

> Love has hands to help others.
> It has feet to hasten to the poor and needy.
> It has eyes to see misery and want.

It has ears to hear the sighs and sorrow of men.
This is what love looks like.

This kind of love is truly beautiful in God's eyes!

An Invitation to Beauty

It's wonderful—and worthy—to excel in different areas.
Maybe you can read the classics like the wind. Maybe
you know so much about math you can tutor most of
your classmates. Maybe you practice your instrument
two hours a day and made first chair. Maybe you bear
the title head cheerleader. Maybe you've mastered a
foreign language. Maybe you are so smart and have
worked so hard you've been granted a scholarship to
college. These are all fantastic achievements. Wonderful!
And they speak loudly of the many character qualities
you possess that were involved in your success.

But...God highly values this great mark of beauty in
your life—mercy. More than any virtue we've looked
at so far, mercy reflects the presence of the Lord in
your heart and life. Mercy adds the lovely fragrance
of the Lord to who you are and to all you do. Mercy
pleases the Lord and is beautiful in His eyes. I'm praying right now that you are asking God to help you be
generous, helpful, compassionate, and merciful. To be
a truly beautiful-in-the-Lord woman who delights (and
excels!) in giving to those who need a helping hand.
Do it—in the name of the Lord!

Study Questions

Using your Bible, read through Proverbs 31:10-31. Then write out verse 20 here:

In this chapter, we talked about a heart that obeys God's Word and does what the Bible says. Look at these verses in your Bible and note what God is saying you should do about those in need.

Moses' Law in Deuteronomy 15:7-8—

Micah 6:8—

Proverbs 11:25—

Proverbs 19:17—

Proverbs 22:9—

What was the most exciting truth or information you discovered in this chapter?

How did this chapter challenge you to pay more attention to growing in mercy?

12

An Eye on the Future

Your Preparation

"When it snows, she has no fear for her household;
for all of them are clothed in scarlet.
She makes coverings for her bed;
she is clothed in fine linen and purple."

PROVERBS 31:21-22

Jesus proclaimed in His famous Sermon on the Mount that no person ever wore clothes as splendid and grand as those worn by King Solomon (Matthew 6:29).

True. But hey, the family of the Proverbs 31 woman may have come close.

We already know quite a few facts about the woman we are examining in Proverbs 31. We know she's a hard worker. We know she gathers wool and flax. We know she processes these raw products until they become yarn.

And now in verses 21-22 we get to see what she makes with that yarn. Here we discover that she weaves, designs, and constructs garments until "her household...are clothed with scarlet" and "she makes coverings for her bed."

Imagine the scene. She and her family live in a desert climate.

It's hot in the summer, but winter brings cold weather and occasional snow. However, no worries—she's prepared. She's been spending time along the way weaving garments to keep her loved ones warm. Yet she goes a step further: She sends them out on the bleak streets dressed like royalty—in *scarlet* wool clothing. I mean, they are wearing one-of-a-kind masterpieces! And she cares for many other needs they have in the home.

Planning for the Future

It's a fact—it snows in Israel! I had a hard time imagining this while Jim and I experienced the extreme heat during our studies in the Holy Land. As we hiked the dry, barren hills, our biggest worry was carrying enough drinking water. We could have cared less about what we were wearing or how we looked! Even though I have a picture clipped out of the *Los Angeles Times* of devout Jews worshiping at Jerusalem's wailing wall in a foot of snow, I still struggled to imagine snow in Israel.

God's Proverbs woman knows that snow comes to her homeland. And she counts on it. But "she has no fear for her household" (Proverbs 31:21). Why? Because she's prepared for the future, come what may. With a keen eye looking ahead, she makes sure she provides what's needed for her family. Verse 21 tells us "all of them are clothed with scarlet," and verse 22 adds that she makes "coverings" for the beds.

For 11 chapters we've witnessed this woman's wisdom, her willingness, her ability to plan ahead, and her management tactics. We know she's a planner who's always thinking about the future. Long before a single tiny snowflake ever appeared, a scene like this occurred:

Rising early one morning Ms. P31 grabs her to-do list and jots several "Notes to Self":

— Prepare for winter.

— Get wool.

— Locate red dye.

— Spin yarn.

— Weave fabric.

— Make winter coats and bed coverings.

This is how work is accomplished. Thinking about the future, plus making lists, plus gathering the needed supplies, equals preparation. Now you're ready to dive into your projects and bring them to life—to make them become reality.

House Beautiful

Proverbs 31:22 says, "She makes coverings for her bed." This reference to coverings actually extends to other home furnishings as well. Some Bible translators have called these furnishings carpets, woven coverlets, and upholstery.[1] One version (which makes me chuckle) even says, "She makes her own quilts."[2]

We know Ms. P31 is creative. And we know that processing yarn and weaving clothes is extremely time-consuming. But what does she do with her leftover yarn, fabric, creativity, and energy? Why, she makes a variety of items for her home— items like pillows, blankets, cushions, drapes, rugs, wall hangings, tablecloths, runners, mats, and upholstery. We can be sure her handiwork brightened up their desert home made of colorless stone.

Room Check

Before we go any further, let's take a look around your place. Let's do a room check. Even if you share a room, you can check out your space.

Check #1: Pretend you're a visitor—Walk through the place where you live. What do you see? What would a guest notice? What mood does your room or space invite? What pleases you about what you see—and what would you like to improve? Are there any eyesores? Clutter? As a homemaker-in-the-making—the keeper of your very own room or space—you are in the position to create a welcoming atmosphere and beautiful environment.

Check #2: Plan several improvements—God's beautiful woman was certainly a do-it-yourselfer! Keep that in mind as you take inventory of your room. What projects are you working on? Do your windows need a good cleaning? How do the walls and floor look?

Not all improvements cost money. In fact, the greatest improvement of all can be making your bed, or cleaning up and removing clutter. For example, you could clean out your closet as soon as you finish this chapter. Or, you could put away things that are lying on your bed, on the floor, a chair, or anywhere else. Also, think about these easy instant improvements: Putting a single flower in a bud vase, rearranging your furniture, adding knickknacks to your bookshelf, using some personal treasures and souvenirs or crafts to add your signature touch and unique flair to your room.

Check #3: Put in some overtime—As in overtime *at home,*

not at the mall! Set aside a Saturday or an evening or two for creating order or working on room-improvement projects.

Wherever your place is for you, it's an expression of you—your virtues, your abilities, your creativity. You may not be able to determine the kind of home your parents provide for you, but you can determine to some extent what your space looks like. Think about it. You control whether it's clean, organized, and orderly…or not. Just taking care of these three actions will make your place a place you want to be and can be proud of.

Talk things over with Mom and Dad. Ask if it's okay for you to do a little redecorating in your room. Maybe Mom will go shopping with you for a few new items for your room. Your parents will probably be thrilled with your interest in your room.

A Touch of Class

And now for our Proverbs lady's clothes.

First we see in verse 22 that "she is clothed in fine linen and purple." Realize that our heroine doesn't have a closet full of clothes. She has a few quality items, each of which took her months (maybe even up to a year) to make for herself. We're not surprised to see that she gives her clothing a touch of class. What she wears is simply regal, fit for royalty. Her clothing is a reflection of her character.

Hmmm, clothes that are purple. For something to be purple means it was colored by a rare and costly dye extracted in minute quantities from a shellfish found on the eastern shores of the Mediterranean Sea.[3] Ever the trader, we can imagine our P31 gal probably exchanged her creative handiwork for this rare, expensive dye when the merchant ships came in.

How to Be Beautiful—Inside and Out

Oh boy! Clothes? Oh yeah—let's go shopping! Anyone want to go to the mall?

Yet there were no malls for the Proverbs 31 woman. Providing clothes and bed coverings for her family wasn't so easy as going to the store. Instead, everyone's wardrobe—including her own—had to be made from scratch with her own hands. This took a l-o-t of her time. And she had to plan ahead to make it all happen.

Though our P31 lady lived in a very different place and time, there are still plenty of lessons from verses 21-22 that you can put into practice in your own life—lessons we see illustrated by her wonderful example.

1. Take care of your clothes. As a modern-day girl, you don't have to sew and weave your clothes. But the clothes you do have should be important to you. Do you wash, dry, fold, hang up, and put your clothes away? I know in some homes, Mom wants to do all the laundry. And in other households, Mom wants each child to learn how to take care of their personal laundry. You want to do what your mom wants you to do. But be sure to ask her to show you how to do it yourself. That's a good way to prepare for your future when you no longer live at home.

2. Think about your future needs—Have you got a physical calendar or planner? Or maybe you use your phone, tablet, or computer for your master calendar. Whatever you use, try to lay out a one-year calendar and then determine your future needs.

When it comes to your clothes, there are a few key times you'll need to think about. Back-to-school clothes, clothes for Easter, for Christmas, and special events. Clothes for summer camp or your family vacation. These are all exciting times that probably call for some cool shopping adventures with Mom. (Yes!)

And how about the clothes you already have? Maybe you need to clean out your closet and drawers and pass on what you've outgrown, or what's ruined, or put out-of-season clothes wherever Mom wants them.

Mark your future events and needs on your calendar. Like our P31 woman, your goal is to look forward with an eye on the future and prepare!

3. Take care of your inner beauty—The woman who is beautiful in God's eyes models His standards in every area of her life, including her choices in clothing. Take a look at some of the standards God sets in His Word.

Just a heads up: Some of the upcoming words or terms may sound a bit old or old-fashioned. Well, they are old because they appear in the Bible. But they are not old-fashioned because "the counsel of the LORD *stands forever*, the plans of His heart *to all generations*"—and that includes you (Psalm 33:11 NKJV). Nothing changes with God. His standards are His standards—period. Here we go!

— *Modest*. First Timothy 2:9 says God's girls of all ages are to "dress modestly." This means clothing that is appropriate for a young woman who's following God. So avoid extremes—not too little, and not too much. Not too skimpy, tight, and revealing, and not too gaudy or expensive. Not too much jewelry, not too much makeup…you get the picture. Your clothes should be stylish, but modest. They should not call attention to your body, but to your godly character. Be stylish…but modest.

— *Decent*. First Timothy 2:9 continues to say "dress… with decency." In other words, be respectable in what you wear. You can respect yourself by what you put on, and others can respect you as well. Set a standard—God's standard of decency—for what you wear.

— *Proper*. Once again 1 Timothy 2:9 sets another criteria: "dress…[with] propriety." The meaning here is to wear what is proper, correct, and right for the occasion. Ask yourself before you leave home, "Is what I'm wearing going to bring honor to Jesus?"

— *Parents*. Throughout the Bible children are told to honor and submit to their parents. This means you won't wear anything your parents haven't approved.

— *Good deeds*. Here's another clothing tip from 1 Timothy 2:9 and 10. God's girl does not want to make her personal life statement with flashy clothes. No, she wants to make her personal life statement through her good deeds. She wants to be known as a girl who's quick to offer a helping hand to others. "Good deeds"—not her clothes—describes how her inner beauty reveals itself to others.

— *Gentle and quiet spirit.* Inner beauty also reveals itself not just in what you do as good deeds, but also how you act. First Peter 3:4 calls this "the lasting beauty of a gentle and quiet spirit, which is very precious in God's sight" (NRSV). Now *that's* beauty!

An Invitation to Beauty

At first glance, a chapter on clothing and being prepared for future needs doesn't look terribly important—or exciting, does it? But it is—for a number of reasons. First, God has put Proverbs 31:21-22 in the Bible. That means these two verses are teaching things God wants you to know. And second, in Ms. P31, God is giving you an example to follow. Her example is His gift to you.

And third, here in verses 21-22, God shines His spotlight on the character trait of preparation—planning and acting ahead so you are prepared for the future. Whew! What a great feeling that is!

Study Questions

Using your Bible, read through Proverbs 31:10-31. Then write out verses 21-22 here:

What do these verses say about clothing? Also note whether the verses refer to physical clothing or inner clothing.

Verse 21—

Verse 22—

Verse 25—

In your Bible, read 1 Timothy 2:9-10. What words does your version of the Bible use to describe God's instruction for your appearance?

What was the most exciting truth or information you discovered in this chapter?

How did this chapter challenge you with regard to your wardrobe and to preparing and planning for the future?

13

A Man of Influence

Your Future Husband

*"Her husband is respected at the city gate,
where he takes his seat among the elders of the land."*

PROVERBS 31:23

Oh no, is this another verse about marriage? I can only imagine what you may be thinking as you look at this chapter title and the verse above! Just let me say one more time that I realize you are probably not married.

And maybe, depending on your age, you aren't even thinking about being a wife. After all, you've still got a lot of growing up to do. And a lot of fun you want to have with friends. Finishing high school is right up there at the top of your list of goals. Maybe you're contemplating college and trying to decide what kind of college—a university? A community college? A technical school? You may even be looking into a variety of careers or professions.

So marriage is more than likely the farthest thing from your mind right now. However, statistics tell us that in the long run, most women marry and have a family. If there's a chance that might be true of your future, then a look at what an awesome husband our P31 woman had won't hurt, will it?

Marriage to a Man of Influence

At this point in Proverbs 31, we finally learn something about the husband of God's beautiful woman. We were introduced to him in verse 11 as a trusting husband who rests his soul safely upon the character of his beautiful-in-God's-eyes wife.

A quick review of verses 10-15 reveals he's the fortunate man she is committed to doing good to all the days of her life. We've witnessed the meals she prepares for him, as well as her management of his home and her contribution to the family finances. And, thanks to her handiwork, he is splendidly clothed in scarlet (verse 21).

"Who can find a virtuous wife?" verse 10 asks (NKJV). Well, this guy has. God has definitely graced him with one of His truly beautiful-on-the-inside women.

Going to Work

In addition to being richly blessed by God through his wife, this man is himself a blessing to many. You see, he is a man of influence. Let me explain.

The verse for this chapter says, "Her husband is known in the gates, when he sits among the elders of the land" (NKJV). This may not sound like a big deal, but it's actually huge! In the days of the Proverbs 31 woman, cities were walled all around for protection. The only way people, animals, and goods could enter and exit the city was through the gates.

These gated entrances contained large rooms built into the city wall. Some of the walls had compartments that were set aside as guard rooms, complete with a well for water, a place for a fire, and inside steps leading up to the top of the wall. Other chambers served as official government offices.

On the Job

And exactly what happened in the gates as the townspeople passed through them in their daily comings and goings? In the coolness and protection of these stone rooms, legal and governmental decisions were made. Deliberations took place. Political issues were settled. Official proclamations and edicts were read. Matters of public welfare were transacted. Judgments were administered. And legal questions were decided.

This is the place where the husband of the Proverbs 31 woman is "known" as a reputable man who "sits among the elders of the land." Recognized as a leader, he is in a position to influence the life of the community. He may have been an able counselor. He may have been one of the elders who met daily in the town gate to transact public business and decide cases that were brought before them.[1]

Whatever the specific situation, we see that Mr. P31 is well-known because he sits in the council chambers. With other respected civic leaders, he conducts legal business.[2] He is an honored citizen who is held in high esteem by the townspeople and the officials of his community. He is most definitely a man of influence.

Who Can Find a Godly Man?

I've heard it said, "If you want to find a godly man, start by being a godly woman." Well, I've got great news. Meet Ruth! Her story in the Bible shows us an example of a godly woman and her courtship with a godly man.

And now, meet Boaz, the man who ultimately became Ruth's husband. By being an example of what I call a Proverbs 31 man, this godly guy was the type of man who took notice of Ruth, a godly gal. Because he was a man of character, he noticed Ruth, a woman of character. Take a look at a few of Boaz's character qualities. He was:

Godly—He had a passion for God. (Boaz asked God to bless Ruth—Ruth 2:12.)

Diligent—He had a willingness to work. (Boaz was a careful manager of his property—2:1.)

Friendly—He had a desire to be friendly. (Boaz gave a warm greeting to his workers and welcomed Ruth to his field—2:4,8.)

Merciful—He had compassion for others. (Boaz asked about Ruth's situation and acted on her behalf—2:7.)

Encouraging—He desired to contribute positively to others. (Boaz pointed out Ruth's strong qualities and spoke of them to encourage her—2:12.)

Generous—He had a giving heart. (Although Ruth needed food and was willing to work for it, Boaz gave her extra—2:15.)

Kind—He had a kind heart. (Naomi thanked God for Boaz's kindness toward her and Ruth—2:20.)

Discreet—He had a desire to protect Ruth's reputation. (Boaz sent Ruth home from the threshing floor before daylight—3:14.)

Faithful—He was a man who was true to his word. (Boaz followed through on his promise to marry Ruth—4:1-10.)

This portrait of Boaz, a man of influence, should give you a better understanding of what the husband of the Proverbs 31 woman was like. Oh, and while you're looking and waiting for Prince Charming, this list defines what any guy you are interested in should be like, and especially what any man you are considering marrying should be.

Behind Every Good Man

When I think about the husband and wife pictured in Proverbs 31 (as well as Boaz and Ruth), I think of them as being like a pair of bookends. Both of them were pillars in the community, both were known in the city gate (verses 23 and 31), and both were committed to the good of others (verses 20 and 23).

Although their spheres of influence were different and at opposite ends of who they influenced and ministered to, they both exhibited the same virtuous character traits. They both lived for God with the same purpose—serving others. Just as Solomon wisely noted, "Two are better than one" (Ecclesiastes 4:9). Take a look at how the husband and wife in Proverbs 31 worked together as a couple…just like a pair of bookends!

The Proverbs 31 Bookends

✤ He contributes to the community.
   She is his helper (Genesis 2:18).

✤ He is successful in the realm of city management.
   She is successful in the realm of family and home management.

❀ He is happy at work.
  She is happy working at home.

❀ He is respected and held in high esteem.
  She preserves and advances his honor by her conduct and example.

❀ He is deferred to as a solid, influential citizen.
  She brings credit to him.

❀ He is a counselor, a man of common sense and not-so-common insight.
  She speaks with loving wisdom.

❀ He exerts his influence on the life of the community in the city gates.
  She influences the community from home.

❀ He is known for his solid character and important contributions.
  So is she.

❀ He has achieved some worldly wealth and social status.
  She improves his financial situation as well as his social standing by what she is to him and what she does for him as a wife.

❀ He has reached his professional aims.
  She has helped him do so by her diligence and frugality.

❀ He has earned prestige.
  She is respected for her creative handiwork.

❊ He is a virtuous man.
   She is a virtuous woman.

❊ He is crowned with honor.
   She is his crown (Proverbs 12:4).[3]

How to Be Beautiful—Inside and Out

By now you've gotten to know the Proverbs 31 woman pretty well. And you've met Ruth, another woman in the Bible who was called a "virtuous woman" or a "woman of excellence."

What was it about Ruth's activities that made her so special? Here's a brief look at her life. As you read, notice the similarities to the Proverbs 31 woman. Then check your life against theirs. Jot down answers to the questions to revisit later and make changes and adjustments

Ruth's Character Qualities   **Also Seen in Proverbs 31**

1. Devoted to her family
   Ruth 1:15-18   Proverbs 31:10-12,23
How are your relationships at home?

2. Delighting in her work

    Ruth 2:2   Proverbs 31:13

What is your attitude toward your responsibilities? For instance, do you grumble? Make excuses? What can you do differently?

3. Diligent in her labor

    Ruth 2:7,17,23   Proverbs 31:14-21,24,27

What is your attitude toward work? Do you tend to be lazy, to put off work, or do you dive in and do it?

4. Dedicated to godly speech

    Ruth 2:10,13   Proverbs 31:26

What are your favorite topics to talk about? Do you need to choose some better ones? Like what?

5. Dependent on God

    Ruth 2:12   Proverbs 31:25b,30

How is your prayer life. Are you giving God your burdens?

6. Dressed with care

Ruth 3:3   Proverbs 31:22,25a

How does your style check out against God's guidelines for modest and moderation?

7. Discreet with men

Ruth 3:6-13   Proverbs 31:11-12,23

Are you going slow and being careful in your relation-ships with guys? Have you made a list of standards to use in evaluating guy-friends?

_____ Check here when you've made your list.

I hope you'll carve out about ten minutes in your busy day to read through the book of Ruth. It's only four chapters in the Bible, but it's a beautiful love story of two people who weren't necessarily considered to be beautiful from a worldly viewpoint. No, they were better than all that—they were two godly people who married…and were blessed by God to be in the bloodline of David—and Jesus.

An Invitation to Beauty

When it comes to being beautiful on the outside, your genes definitely come into play. And so does taking care of yourself through cleanliness, good grooming, and health. But inner beauty is all about your heart—what you are putting into it, what you are feeding it, and how tightly you are guarding it.

The Proverbs 31 woman was a walking, breathing example of every single letter and stanza of the alphabetical rhyme that makes up chapter 31 of Proverbs. And what does God show us? What does He allow us to see? Her character! Twenty-plus traits that let us know she loved the Lord and belonged to Him.

Only God knows if you will marry someday. But it helps to remember that an awesome woman will catch the attention of an awesome man. A godly woman will attract a godly man—a man of character. But best of all, a godly woman, whether single or married, will please the Lord. *She* will be praised (verse 31)—by all who know her, and best of all, by God Himself.

Study Questions

Using your Bible, read through Proverbs 31:10-31. Then write out verse 23 here:

With the Proverbs 31:23 man and Boaz in mind, create a list of character qualities you know God wants you to look for in a man—that is, any man you would spend time with dating or in a courtship, and definitely any man you would consider marrying. Use your journal, the back inside cover of this book, even a special document you save on your computer or in a notebook or special file folder. Write it out. Pray it to God. Commit to it. File it. And look at it often. Purpose to wait for true love—God's kind of love—until you meet Mr. Right.

When you make your list, it will be helpful to look again at these two lists in this chapter, "Boaz, Man of Character" and the man's role in "The Proverbs 31 Bookends."
_____ Check here when you are finished making your list.

What was the most exciting truth or information you discovered in this chapter?

How did this chapter challenge you as a young single woman to focus on inner beauty?

14

A Dream to Pursue

Your Industry

*"She makes linen garments and sells them,
and supplies the merchants with sashes."*

PROVERBS 31:24

I'm sure you've seen this scene before—a group of young girls sitting at a makeshift table out at the curb in front of a house. And once you stopped to check it out, you discovered they were selling lemonade, or homemade cookies, or both. Maybe you've been one of these industrious girls. Well, these girls are taking first steps into a "business" venture.

Everyone loves hearing the success stories of artists and entrepreneurs. And I'm no different. In fact, I have folders full of these remarkable tales. Whenever I hear about a woman our society labels "successful," I wonder, *How did it happen? What steps did she take? Where did her knowledge and skills come from? And her ideas?*

Amazingly, as each woman's story unfolds, two common essentials for success emerge: She developed *something personal* into *something professional.*

Many of my friends fit this description of success. They are energetic and always busy, pursuing new information about their small business dream. They love what they do—interior decorating, food preparation and catering, crafts, quilting, or photography. Others do bookkeeping, tax preparation, or teach art or music lessons in their home. These women love being busy and creative, and are happy to teach others how to do the same thing.

I realize that what I see these friends doing and accomplishing today didn't spring up yesterday. No, they've been at it for years. Since childhood they've tried a variety of ventures. They've moved through a number of hobbies. Maybe they even set up a lemonade stand or two…or twenty!

In time and through trial and error and elimination, they zeroed in on one special skill or endeavor and focused their time and effort on that one activity. It's no surprise, then, that over time they excelled and became experts.

They turned something personal—a passion, an ability, a dream—into something professional. They enjoy sharing what they know or can do. They love bettering the lives of others, bringing joy and encouragement and needed skills to those they know and work with. They may even earn a little income that helps contribute to their family's needs, or to covering the cost of a missions trip, or to some special supplies for their hobby.

What skills and talents has God given to you? What knowledge do you possess? You are blessed with many abilities and aptitudes! And you can bless others with your expertise. There are people out there who want to know what you know. Who want to do what you can do. It's quite possible that you can turn your something personal—your very own talent and passion—into something professional.

Of course, the ultimate woman for you to model after is God's Proverbs 31 woman. Take a closer look at her skills and industry.

The Birth of a Business

Just as the pattern in a piece of wood repeats itself in cut after cut, so weaving is ingrained in the soul of the Proverbs 31 woman. It's definitely her "thing." Just look at the number of times it's mentioned in the 22 verses we're going through:

> She seeks wool and flax for her fabrics (verse 13).
> She sits up late processing her raw materials into yarn by candlelight (verses 18-19).
> She gives her warm, handmade garments to the poor (verse 20).
> She regally decks out her family, her home, and herself with her handiwork (verses 21-22).

And now we can add another verse: "She makes linen garments and sells them, and supplies the merchants with sashes" (verse 24).

Moving systematically through this poem of praise, you can't help but notice that this lady's business began at home. All she was doing was working hard and taking care of her family. And, as her skills grew and improved, others began to notice and want her products. Soon her efforts spilled out of the home and into her community.

A little more research reveals that she created an industry that reached to the markets of the known world. In her day, the goods she created with her hands would have been carried by merchant ships and camel caravans to the ends of the earth.

The fact that "she makes linen garments and sells them, and supplies the merchants with sashes" tells us a lot about the quality of her work. Merchants who did business with traders in other lands wanted her goods so they could sell them. She was definitely a creative professional. How did it happen? Why, something personal became something professional! Something she dreamed of doing and loved doing became so excellent she became a professional at it.

The Expression of Creativity

"She makes linen garments." What was the process of creating linen fabric so that it could become a garment?

First, Ms. P31 made the linen fabric itself, and then she made the clothes from it. The fineness of her linen made it soft and usable for bedclothes, undergarments, or lightweight tunic-like smocks worn in the summer on a bare body. Her linen garments were soft, thin, and fine—and therefore costly.

This woman's handiwork also included sashes, and next we see that she "supplies the merchants with sashes." Like a belt or girdle, a sash was worn to gather up the flowing garments (like those still worn in Israel today). Once a person's garments were tied up with a sash, physical work was much easier to do. Leather belts were common, but a linen sash or belt was much more attractive and more costly. They were often woven with gold and silver thread, and studded with jewels and gold. These were the stunning works of art our lady supplied to the merchants.

The Enrichment of Estate

Here's another lesson from the Proverbs 31 woman: "She makes linen garments *and sells them*." Knowing and being confident that her merchandise is good, she moves her handmade goods out from the home and into the local markets.

Once out of her home, her goods were picked up from the local markets by Canaanite and Phoenician traders and taken to distant lands by caravan and ship. These traders only chose the best, the most exquisite, the most extraordinary goods to carry to foreign markets. Well, our P31 woman's sashes certainly qualified! She was ever the businesswoman—trading, exchanging, bartering, and selling her sashes and linen garments.

I don't want you to get discouraged by this woman's success if you don't feel like you've found an area yet in which you excel. Just keep these two points in mind as you pursue your dreams:

❀ *Don't neglect your responsibilities.* Be sure you take care of your relationships and duties at home, your schoolwork, and any other commitments you have. Your responsibilities come first—*then* work on your projects.

❀ *Give it time.* Start small. Watch for pockets of time you can fill with your projects. You can laze around and watch another TV program, or you can slip into your room and do your thing. Or you can work on your project on a table near the TV set. That way, you are still with the family and joining in on their activity, but you are making progress on your goals to develop skills.

Also, make a habit of carrying items that you need for working on your projects in your backpack or a cute bag. You probably spend a lot of time waiting, a lot of time in the car. Just pull out your knitting or writing notebook or beads— even a book or magazine that has information you can learn from—and enjoy.

Give it time, and give it time each day. A little time each day adds up over a lifetime. Doing something each day ultimately adds up to something very special. One of my favorite quotes promises that "fifteen minutes a day devoted to one definite study will make one a master in a dozen years."[1]

How to Be Beautiful—Inside and Out

Once you identify what your "thing" is, you're ready to go, ready to move forward! To start spreading your wings in your new adventure, here are a few keys to fueling your excitement and expanding your skills.

1. Stay alert—Start noticing what others are doing that is creative. And keep up with what's happening in your area of interest. Try to stay on the cutting edge of your thing.

2. Don't forget to plan—Use your spare minutes to plan and create in your mind, to think about ideas, designs, story-lines. Make a mental shopping list of items you need so you can move forward on your project…and start saving your money. Learn to plan rather than zone out. While you're wait-ing in all those checkout lines, plan! Keep your mind thinking about how to do what you want to do, and how to do it better.

3. Take the initiative—It takes initiative to make the phone call to enroll in a class or join a group that will help you develop your skills. It takes initiative to go to a specialty store and purchase a magazine that targets your area of creativity. It takes initiative to subscribe to a journal, magazine, newspaper, or educational cable class that will help you in your creative pursuits. It takes initiative to bring your dreams down to earth and finally set up a work station, the sewing machine, or the easel. It takes initiative to find out where to send your samples of greeting cards, your manuscript, your book ideas, or your magazine article. It takes initiative to enter your sketch or watercolor or painting in an art show. It takes initiative to attend a demonstration that addresses your area of interest and desired expertise. What first step will you take?

4. Work hard—Hard work? Well, that's a given. Hard work is essential for success in any venture, but you'll love the results!

An Invitation to Beauty

God is the creator of the universe. And He created man in His image. That means you, as one of His masterpieces, are creative. There is some avenue through which you can express the creative gifts and talents God has given you. Don't forget to ask Him to lead and guide you to discover your special area of creativity.

Study Questions

Using your Bible, read through Proverbs 31:10-31. Then write out verse 24 here:

Read Exodus 35:25-26. God had told Moses to build a tabernacle (or large tent) as a place where God Himself could dwell with His people.

—Who do you see involved in this work?

—What were they doing?

—What was their motivation?

Read Acts 9:36-39.

—Who is the woman featured here, and what is she
known for according to verse 36?

—What does verse 39 say was one of her specialties?

—To learn the exciting conclusion, read verses 40-41!
What happened?

What was the most exciting truth or information you discovered in this chapter?

How did this chapter challenge you to pursue your
dreams and bless others?

15

A Wardrobe of Virtues

Your Core Values

"She is clothed with strength and dignity;
she can laugh at the days to come."

PROVERBS 31:25

What does your daily startup time look like? I'm pretty sure you get up. Maybe you just wake up, or maybe you use an alarm…or maybe Mom is your alarm.

Okay, so you get up. Then what?

As we've moved through the Proverbs 31 woman's day, we've discovered that she probably spent some time with the Lord in her early morning hours. Hopefully this important wake-up activity is also a part of your daily routine. A young woman who desires to be beautiful in God's eyes wants to look to Him first.

Here's one way of looking at your quiet time. Recently in my women's Sunday school class, someone shared this concept from the little pamphlet *My Heart—Christ's Home*. In it, Christ is speaking to the person who is meeting with Him each morning for a quiet time:

"I will be here every morning early. Meet me here and we will start the day together." One day this person missed his meeting with the Lord, and then another…and another. When he finally returned to spend time with Christ, Jesus said:

"The trouble is that you have been thinking of the quiet time, of Bible study and prayer, as a means for your own spiritual growth. This is true, but you have forgotten that this time means something to me also…At great cost I have redeemed you. I value your fellowship. Just to have you look up into my face warms my heart…Whether or not you want to be with me, remember I want to be with you. I really love you."[1]

Moving on from the miracle of actually getting out of bed and spending time with the Lord, I am guessing that your next step is to get dressed. (How am I doing?) Opening your closet door and rummaging through your drawers, you take a look. "What's here? What's clean? What's not too wrinkled?" As you think through the events scheduled for your new day, you finally choose clothes that fit your activities and finish getting dressed.

With that done, we could say you are now ready to step out of your room and into your day. But there's one more crucial—yet beautiful—kind of garment that should not be forgotten or omitted: the clothing of godly character.

The Clothing of Character

Unlike so many of us today, our P31 lady didn't have a lot of clothing to choose from. In fact, the heavy woolen cloak people wore in her day also served as their blanket at night. But outwardly she was adequately and beautifully clothed with what was needed for her day's work.

More important, however, was the fact she clothed herself inwardly with layer upon layer of good character qualities. To her, they were absolutely essential garments. And these traits are not clothing that hangs in a closet. They are clothing that enhances your core values, clothing for the heart and soul. Inner clothing. The kind of clothing that Proverbs 31:25 speaks of: "Strength and dignity are her clothing" (NASB).

Here we see *strength* as an attribute of God's beautiful woman. We know she has strong arms for doing physical work (verse 17). But she also wears strength of character like a garment. One translation of verse 25 says, "She puts on strength and honor as if they were her clothes" (NIrV).

This quality of strength manifests itself in a variety of ways. For instance:

> She has built up economic strength
> (verses 16,18,24).
> She has built up a strong family unit
> (verses 28-29).
> She has built up a strong reputation
> (verse 29).

Are you wondering where this kind of inner strength comes from? It comes from God. Even though the Bible refers to women as "the weaker vessel" or the weaker sex (see 1 Peter 3:7), a woman of any age who follows God is strong. Well, the Proverbs 31 woman is strong in wisdom. And she's also strong in her knowledge of God. Besides developing physical strength through her daily work, her pure heart and virtues and dignified conduct are marks of her inner strength and core values.

Dignity is another of this woman's beauty marks. The literal Hebrew translation of this term is "splendor."[2] Her noble spirit gave her the aura of majesty. One look at her reveals a display of her virtuous character, her regal bearing, and her godly behavior. All that she is, is touched with the beauty of dignity.

Joy for a Lifetime

And now for the payoff! Clothed in her wardrobe of strength and dignity, this woman will "rejoice in time to come" (NKJV). Hey, she's got no worries! She lives each day with joy. And, in the words of another translation, "she smiles at the future."[3] When she looks ahead through the corridor of time to the future—whether to a new day or to her death—she "can laugh at the days to come."[4] Now that's strength!

Strength and dignity and honor are part of her clothing. In our model woman in Proverbs 31 we see no anxieties, no worries, no fears. Only strength and dignity. She doesn't waste time or energy on guessing or worrying about life's uncertainties.

Whether she's thinking about the past, the present, or the future, it's all good. When she looks backward, she has no regrets. When she looks forward, she has nothing to dread. Living in the present, she knows only the joy of the Lord.

How to Be Beautiful—Inside and Out

I once read that life can be divided into six major areas. As we look at them now, I want you to especially see how strength and honor affect all areas of your life. Take a look at how.

1. Your spiritual life—Oh, how girls of all ages love their closets! But have you heard about a "prayer closet"? Some people use this term to mean a place you retreat to for your quiet time, your prayer time, your time in God's Word. A place where you meet or spend time with the Lord.

It's pretty obvious this is the closet you want to visit first each day. We'll get to Proverbs 31:30 soon, but it stresses that "a woman who fears the LORD, she shall be praised." Before you choose your beautiful clothing for the day, honor God by choosing to meet with Him. There in your quiet time—in your prayer closet—He will beautify you on the inside. He is the only One who can make you genuinely beautiful.

2. Your family life—Whatever your circumstances, you have a family. You have parents, sisters, brothers, grandparents, aunts, uncles, nieces, nephews, and cousins to love. One obvious lesson for you today is that God's excellent woman in Proverbs 31 put her family first (verses 28-29). She knew it… and so did her family members.

So how about this? Each day when you pray, pray for everyone under your roof and any family members who are away from home. Do you realize it's impossible to pray for someone and hate them or neglect them? So pray away. Pray like crazy. Then see how many little ways you can let the people you pray for know that you love them. And if no one notices or says, "Thank you," no problem! As the Bible tells us, "whatever you do, do it heartily, as to the Lord and not to men" (Colossians 3:23 NKJV).

3. Your financial life—Most girls your age have allowances, birthday money, money from babysitting or a part-time job. So the big question is this: What financial plan and goals do you have for your money? Are you giving at church? Are you one of the many who spends every bit of any money you have as soon as you get it? Or do you save it for special projects, sales, or dreams and goals.

Think big. You are no longer a member of the stuffed animal and princess figurines crowd. So set a big goal. Think laptop, tablet, e-reader. Think college. Think enrollment fees for a specialty school or classes that support your hobbies. Think summer missions trip. Set a goal that's big enough to help you say no to little things.

4. Your physical life—(Oh, no! We knew this would come up sooner or later.) It's a fact: Youth and young adults today don't get enough exercise. So follow in our P31 woman's steps and strengthen yourself (see verse 17). Go for a walk each day. Or borrow Mom's treadmill. Join your parents on the next local bridge run or 5K run. (And don't worry, you don't have to run these races—you can be one of the walkers.) Take tennis lessons. Even go bowling! Every little bit of exercise helps.

Food, anyone? Every young woman needs a working knowledge of information regarding health. Check out a book from the library on food groups, calories, and sample diets for health. If you need to lose a few pounds, do it. If you need to put on a few pounds, do it. Your goal is to feel good so you can breeze through your responsibilities and schoolwork and still have enough energy to pursue your dreams.

5. Your mental life—In the Bible, God calls you to love Him with all your mind (Luke 10:27). What you think about is important because it will be reflected in your life, your attitudes, your choices, your behavior, and your speech.

Here's a thought question: How do you usually use your mind? What do you think about…or worry about? And what kinds of thoughts do you think? Negative or positive? Destructive or constructive? Lies and gossip, or truth? Mean or loving? Set a goal to stop your negative thoughts and choose to use your mind in these ways:

— Think about God and His promises and love for you.

— Think about encouraging truths from the Bible.

— Think about plans that will help you meet your commitments, or make a tough decision, or solve a problem, or reach a goal.

— Think about the Proverbs 31 woman and all her many wonderful qualities.

— Think about your Sunday school or Bible study lesson.

— Think about the lyrics to your favorite praise and worship music.

6. *Your social life*—Time with God? Check! Time with family? Check! Time taking care of responsibilities? Check!

Now how about time with your friends? Oh boy! Finally! Now the question is, Who should you be spending time with? The best advice I ever received about "friends" is this: Realize there are those who pull you up, those who pull you along, and those who pull you down. So…

Who are the people who pull you down, who try to tear you away from what is good and right and godly? Obviously these are not the people you want to spend time with.

Who are the people who pull you along, who are trying to follow God and encourage you to do the same? Now we're talking about real friends! Yes, spend as much time with them as you can.

Who are the people who pull you up, mentors or girls a little older than you, who are ahead of you in what it means to be a woman after God's own heart? Definitely spend time with this kind of friend.

I'm sure you already know how important friends and the right kind of friends are. But I hope you grasp that it's also a good thing to be like Jesus, who was a friend to sinners (Luke 7:34), who went about doing good (Acts 10:38). So be friendly to everyone. You don't have to be their best friend, but you can be friendly. You have so much to give, even to the kids you pass in the hall at school. Just about everyone will enjoy—and maybe some will even need—a smile from you, a greeting, a kind word. As the proverb says, "Do not withhold good from those to whom it is due, when it is in your power to act" (Proverbs 3:27). Extend the beauty of your kindness to others.

An Invitation to Beauty

Hopefully you can see how each of these areas in your life can be strengthened so that, like the beautiful woman in Proverbs 31, you can rejoice in each day and in the future. Here are a few "just for today" thoughts:

Just for today...
give your life afresh to God.

Just for today...
show love to your family and be "too nice."

Just for today...
think about how you use your money.

Just for today...
pay attention to what you eat and drink.

Just for today...
grow in character through the choices you make.

Just for today...
reach out and encourage your best friend in her spiritual journey.

Just for tonight...
utter a prayer to God to wake up tomorrow and repeat this plan for your inner beauty.

Study Questions

Using your Bible, read through Proverbs 31:10-31. Then write out verse 25 here:

God tells you exactly what should make up your inner beauty. Look up these verses in your Bible and list the actions and attitudes God tells you to *put off* or rid yourself of…and to *put on* or clothe yourself with.

Colossians 3:8 (look for 5):

—

—

—

—

—

Colossians 3:12 (look for 5):

—

—

—

—

—

Colossians 3:14:

1 Peter 3:4:

1 Peter 5:5:

What was the most exciting truth or information you discovered in this chapter?

How did this chapter challenge you to grow, sharpen, or improve your core values?

A Law of Kindness

Your Words

"She opens her mouth with wisdom,
and on her tongue is the law of kindness."

PROVERBS 31:26 (NKJV)

*A*re you ready for two more beauty marks that set you apart from all others? You may not have all the clothes you want—or the brand names you wish for. And you may not have the color of hair or eyes you would dearly love to have. But these two qualities we're about to discover will send you into warp speed right past most of the people on the planet in the Beauty Department.

As we can see in Proverbs 31:26, they are "wisdom" and "kindness." And here's a heads up for you: These two character qualities will be hard to achieve. That's because to develop them, you will have to learn to control the words that come out of your mouth.

I'm sure you already know firsthand that the tongue can trip you up on your journey toward God's kind of beauty. Beautiful speech requires serious attention. It's a minute-by-minute and word-by-word challenge. As James wrote in his epistle, "Anyone who is never at fault in what they say is perfect" (James 3:2).

And here's another fact: Much of what you've already learned in this book will seem easy when you compare it to speaking with wisdom and kindness. Actions are usually quite easy to master—actions like being organized, getting up early, doing your work at home and school, taking care of your room and clothes, even managing and giving away some of your money. Actions are externals. You can learn what you need to know from books, people, and practice. But your speech is a matter of the heart.

That's what Jesus teaches us. He said, "Out of the abundance of the heart [the] mouth speaks" (Luke 6:45 NKJV). To be truly beautiful in God's eyes, we must *want* to master this next difficult-but-beautiful step toward more godly speech. God wants His wisdom and His kindness to rule over our speech—and our hearts.

Wise in Speech

Let's rewind for a minute and remember who's writing Proverbs 31:10-31. It's a woman. And she's teaching or speaking these 22 verses to her young son. In these verses we see firsthand the wisdom of her speech. She gives 22 verses of pure wisdom and godly instruction. Every single word she is saying will improve your life.

In verse 26 we read, "She opens her mouth with wisdom" (NKJV). So right away, you get an important message. The wording tells you her mouth is not always open! She's not a yapper or a compulsive talker or a jabber-mouth. Unless she has something wise and kind to say, her mouth is shut.

When she does speak, "she opens her mouth with wisdom."

She's wise in what she says, how she says it, and when she says it. Wisdom is defined as "the use of knowledge in a practical and successful way."[1] These words in Proverbs 31 address practical topics people of all ages need to know. So this woman opens her mouth to share wisdom. She pours out practical knowledge for living to her precious son...and to you.

Kind in Heart

Verse 26 continues, and we learn that "on her tongue is the law of kindness." Not only does our P31 lady let wisdom guide her speech, but she also limits what she shares according to the law of kindness. Everything she utters is in the spirit of kindness and in the manner of a kind and gentle heart. She has wisdom and she shares it, but never in a way that hurts the hearer. Her goal is to never hurt a person or be destructive with her words.

Take a mini-break and think about this woman's daily life. She has her husband—and wants to encourage and bless him. She has children—and as a parent she must instruct, train, and discipline them. She has servants who reside in her home—and they need directions each day. She meets merchants and buyers—and must deal with them as she barters, bargains, and buys. To every person in her life, words must be spoken. The Proverbs 31 woman makes sure her words are wise and kind.

Oh, and by the way, if a wife in her day spoke with a loud voice, her husband could divorce her. And how was "loud" measured? If the neighbors could hear her speak while she was in her own house, she was being loud.

Note to self: Dial it down! No loud talking!

The Absence of Evil

What's true in art is also true of speech: What is *not* present can make a louder statement than what is. So let's take a look at what is absent from the words our gal from Proverbs utters.

For starters, there's no gossip, slander, or unkindness toward others. Kindness would never do that.

And there's no complaining. As a woman who fears the Lord (verse 30), she knows God has perfect control over the circumstances of her life. So she really has nothing to complain about! (And hey, neither do you.)

Wit, humor, and jesting—especially at the expense of others—are not how she wants to make her mark.

And she doesn't say anything that is indiscreet—anything that shouldn't be said or is harmful.

Meaningless talk of trivia and trifles? No way. Not for her! She's erased these from her speech too.

Also, as an estate manager and businesswoman, she could speak in an assertive or forceful or bossy manner, but once again, kindness rules her words and reins her in.

Here are a couple bits of wisdom to chew on:

—"Great minds discuss ideas. Average minds discuss events. Small minds discuss people."[2]

—"It is better to bite your tongue than to make a biting remark."[3]

A Fountain of Life

God gives us a great word picture regarding our words and speech and the effect they can have on others. It's in Proverbs 10:11: "The mouth of the righteous is a fountain of life."

The setting of Proverbs 31 is the deadly, dry land of Israel. Hardship was—and still is—the rule of the day. Survival was—and still is—a day in, day out challenge. Brutal heat and life-threatening thirst are two facts of daily life. I wish I could adequately describe how serious and how relentless the people's daily concern about having adequate water is in this parched and waterless land. Believe me, given your choice of food or water, you would always choose water!

As we consider the setting in Israel, the image painted in Proverbs 10:11 comes alive for us: "The mouth of the righteous is a fountain of life." Against the harsh desert background, and knowing how important water is in sustaining life, the writer compares godly speech to life-giving water. He likens the positive effect of godly speech on our emotional needs to the effect of water on our physical needs.

Imagine the classic scene of being a person in a desert who is lost and dying and at last stumbles upon an oasis or a spring. For such a person to find a fountain in the desert is the same as finding life. Likewise, being in the presence of a woman who speaks words of wisdom and kindness is like finding life!

Our words have a ministry to others when they are wise—and kind.

How to Be Beautiful—Inside and Out

I wish I had the space to tell you of the years I've been struggling toward beautiful speech! I can only say that I know God knows how desperately I was trying. And I keep trying because this principle of wise and kind speech is God's will and His clear standard for my life and my lips.

The book of Proverbs, tucked into the middle of your Bible, offers priceless and pertinent eternal wisdom. In it, God has included some rules for godly speech. Read on.

1. Establish two guidelines—God's beautiful woman set two guidelines for her speech: (1) Speak only if the words are wise; and (2) speak only if the words are kind (Proverbs 31:26). By following these two guidelines, you will always have something to say that's worth saying (wisdom). And you will say it in the right way (with kindness). You can know a lot, but if you speak without kindness, your words will be less effective.

2. Think before you speak—"The heart of the righteous studies how to answer, but the mouth of the wicked pours forth evil" (Proverbs 15:28 NKJV). Take time to pause and think about your words before you speak them. Ask yourself: "Is it wise? Is it kind? If it is, I can say it. If it isn't, I shouldn't say it." When you're not careful, evil "gushes like a torrent"![4]

3. Learn to wait—When something unpleasant happens, make it your first "law" to *stop*, and do and say nothing. Do this even if it's only for a few seconds. If you have to respond right away, at least make sure your words are soft. That's a good first step because "a gentle answer turns away wrath, but a harsh word stirs up anger" (Proverbs 15:1). Then wait. Waiting buys you time to:

— Find out what God says about how to handle the situation.

Find out what other wise people say you should

do. As Proverbs 11:14 cautions, "Where there is no counsel, the people fall" (NKJV). Proverbs 28:26 warns, "Those who trust in themselves are fools."

Pray for a kind heart and a wise solution for the problem situation.

— Calm down. Cool down. Back off. As Proverbs 17:27 says, "A man of understanding is of a calm spirit" (NKJV). Only when you are calm will you be able to listen to good counsel and make wise decisions.

Weigh the problem. Decide whether the situation is something you can overlook (Proverbs 19:11), or whether you need to "open" your mouth and speak to the people involved—with wisdom and kindness, of course!

— Consider the person involved. Is the offense out of character, or is it becoming a pattern? Is it a one-time failure, or another in a string of repeated improper behavior?

4. *Add sweetness to your speech*—Wisdom possesses great charm when sweetened with the right words. That truth is found in Proverbs 16:21—"Sweetness of the lips increases learning" (NKJV). Speaking pleasantly will always make others more willing to listen and be instructed. It's true that a spoonful of sugar makes the medicine go down!

5. *Err on the side of less*—When it comes to words, less is always best! Proverbs 10:19 says, "When there are many words, transgression is unavoidable, but he who restrains his

lips is wise" (NASB). Proverbs 17:28 points out that even fools are thought to be wise if they keep silent. In contemporary language, "Better to be quiet and be thought a fool than to speak and remove all doubt!"

An Invitation to Beauty

Your beauty begins with your relationship with Jesus. You can bring His beauty into every situation. And through the words you speak, you can bless and beautify the hearts and lives of others.

Think again about that fountain in the desert, the one that is a fountain of life. Then think of the hurting, stressed, struggling people who fill your world each day. While they may wear brave smiles, another proverb reveals the truth behind such smiles: "The heart knows its own bitterness...Even in laughter the heart may sorrow, and the end of that mirth may be grief" (Proverbs 14:10 and 13 NKJV).

The next time you pray, make a pact with God. Commit yourself to speaking life-giving words when you open your mouth. Speak words that are wise and kind. Speak words that refresh and encourage. Speak words that cheer and uplift.

You can be a fountain of life instead of the person whose words "pierce like swords." Let yours be "the tongue of the wise [that] brings healing" (Proverbs 12:18).

Study Questions

Using your Bible, read through Proverbs 31:10-31. Then write out verse 26 here:

Take some time now to meet Hannah! Read about her in 1 Samuel 1:1-18. How was she treated by Peninnah (verse 6)?

How did Hannah respond to Peninnah? Well, you won't find any evidence of her lashing back with harsh or demeaning comments. And you won't find these two women going into sparring mode, exchanging insults and accusations. What do you see Hannah doing instead in verse 10?

How does Hannah show you a better way to respond when people are mean to you?

How was Hannah treated by the priest, Eli (verse 14)?

How did Hannah respond to Eli's accusations (verses 15-16)?

How does Hannah show you a better way to respond when people misinterpret or misunderstand your actions?

What was the most exciting truth or information you discovered in this chapter?

How did this chapter challenge you to make improvements and changes in the words you speak?

17

A Watchful Eye

Your Management

*"She watches over the ways of her household,
and does not eat the bread of idleness."*

PROVERBS 31:27 (NKJV)

So what did you do today?"

In years past, these were the words of my Jim's cheerful greeting every single day when he arrived home from work. Glad to be home and happily making small talk, he turned his attention my way. How sweet, especially after his trying days at work.

But I have to admit, these words also made my heart race because for some reason, my mind homed straight in on that little word *do*—"So, what did you *do* today?" In no way was Jim asking for a blow-by-blow travelog through my activities, but I'm so geared to accountability myself that I almost automatically answered, "I don't know exactly what I did, but I do know one thing—I never sat down all day long!"

This sounds amazing to me even as I'm sharing it, because believe me, caring about how I spend my time hasn't always been true of me! But that was before I learned one dyna-mite lesson from Proverbs 31, a lesson about time and life management: a wise woman "watches over the ways of her household, and does not eat the bread of idleness" (Prov-erbs 31:27 NKJV). The wisdom from this one verse showed me exactly what I should do and not do. It gave me a double-barreled challenge for a lifetime.

Keeping Watch Over Her Responsibilities

"She watches over the ways of her household." We don't know whether or not Ms. P31 had any sheep. But we do know she tended and cared for her "flock" at home—her husband, her children, even her servants. Yes, she had the finances for servants (verse 15), but that didn't keep her from being actively involved in the hands-on management of her house-hold. No one runs her home for her. It's her home, her family, her household, and she considers its management an area of her stewardship. It's her responsibility. And she diligently and fiercely watched over all that was hers.

There's a word picture here you'll love. We know the woman teaching this information is the mother of a prince who would one day be king. So here she uses an image her young son would be familiar with—the fact that one day he will "watch over" his people. She describes his ideal future wife as being like a watchman.

The young prince had grown up seeing watchmen sta-tioned 24 hours a day on the city walls, watchtowers, and hill-tops. A watchman guarded and watched over a city or a field. He was a lookout, ever on the alert for any threats or problems. Any suspicious activity was immediately reported to the king.

The prince knew exactly what a watchman was and what a watchman did. So he probably got the message his mother was sending—he should look for a woman who would "watch over" his family and household affairs, a woman with—as the expression goes—eyes in the back of her head!

"Eyes in the back of her head." What a great picture of the watcher. Like him, she turns her head, looking everywhere so she doesn't miss a single detail. She stands guard, moving her eyes back and forth to see who is coming and who is going. She's the chief overseer of her family and property. You can be sure she kept a close watch over everything.

And she's thorough. "She [looks] well to the ways of her household" (KJV). She doesn't just glance over things or check the temperature at home once in a while. No, she's fierce about her family and property. She personally oversees everything that pertains to her home. You might say she's got her finger on the pulse of her household. Nothing escapes her. You see, her job assignment from God is to take care of her home—the people and the place.

And "she watches over the ways of her household." She watches the patterns of her home life—the "ways" of her household, the habits and activities of the people at home. The Old Testament Hebrew word translated "ways" refers to literal tracks made by constant use, and our P31 woman is constantly aware of these habits and any changes in habits. Nothing blindsides her.

Keeping Watch Over Herself

We're not surprised to learn that the woman who is beautiful in God's eyes also watches over herself: "She...does not

eat the bread of idleness" (NKJV). She chooses not to live a lei-
surely life. As one who vigilantly watches over her household,
she has no place for idleness in her schedule. How could she
afford to be idle? Why, she'd never get her work done and
her responsibilities taken care of. She's got all the busyness
going of just managing her house and watching over her flock.
There's no way she has time to laze around and loaf, neglect-
ing her obligations.

This truth could also be flipped: Because she is not idle,
she has all the time she needs to keep an eye on her home,
her family, and her work. She can be sure everything is managed well.

How to Be Beautiful—Inside and Out

We've gained a lot of insights from all the cultural pictures,
biblical history, and Hebrew meanings we've looked at. All
this information helps you to understand the teaching of Proverbs 31:27. But now let's apply it to you, to your life.

The people at home—Okay, I'm assuming you are probably
not married and don't have a bunch of children or enterprises
to watch over and micromanage. But you do live some-
where—that's your home. And there are people, probably
some family, who also live there.

A good principle to remember when it comes to life under
your roof is "The people first, then the place." The people (yes,
even the pesky ones) who make up your family will always
be vitally important to you. And you can "watch over" them
in a variety of ways.

How about Mom? Wow, if you are fortunate enough to
have a mom who cares, who keeps an eye on you, maybe

even more than you want or appreciate, who gives you work chores, who checks up on you and maybe even nags a little—thank God for her! Be extremely grateful to have her as your mom. Realize she is living out this verse describing the most excellent woman, the woman who is beautiful in God's eyes, the woman who is doing what God wants her to do as a mom. Appreciate her, study her, learn from her, copy her, and tell her "I love you, Mom"… at least several times a day!

You know what her busy life is like, so pray for her—her commitments, her job, her relationship with the Lord. Pray to be a P31 daughter. And don't forget to ask her how her day went—how her commitments and appointments worked out. Remember, you cannot hate or neglect the person you are praying for!

Can you think of ways to sort of "watch over" Mom? Could she use some help in the kitchen? Setting or clearing the table? Running a load of laundry for her, or at least moving it from the washer to the dryer—maybe even folding it? See yourself as her right-hand helper.

You already know she gets tired, so how about asking if there is anything she needs or you could get her (like a cup of coffee!) before you rush out of the house? Is there anything you can do to help? If you drive, can you run any errands for her? And, hey, you can always volunteer to give her a nice neck and shoulder rub!

Maybe the best way you can help your mom oversee the running of the home is to do whatever she asks or tells you to do…when she tells you to. And here's a great habit you can make yours immediately: Whenever she tells you to do anything, say, "Sure!" (And that's with a smile and melody in your voice.) You may need to talk over when she needs it done, but your positive "Sure!" will improve the entire atmosphere in your home.

If you are reading this book, you technically fall into the "Young Adult" category. So I'm assuming you have already given up the brattiness often exhibited by kids and little kids. You are taking on more adult behavior. And with that comes a willingness to think outside of yourself, an initiative to work, to be a self-starter, to help others, to assist your parents—not oppose them and be their #1 problem, their #1 headache, their #1 thorn in the flesh. Be a young woman after God's own heart, who is a daughter after God's own heart too!

How about Dad? There's not a dad on the planet who doesn't love his girls and love a hug and an "I love you, Dad!" at least once a day. And it's even better if you can add "…and you rock, Dad!" So…how can you "watch over" Dad?

Like with Mom, you can volunteer to work alongside him—planting the garden, caring for the lawn, getting the trash out, painting, building, washing the car…and since you are or will be driving a car, it never hurts to learn a little about what's under the hood of the car! You can bake his favorite cookies… just for him from you. You can put a little note into his bag whenever he travels.

And how about this? Try to make it easy on Dad when he has to deliver some bad news to you, like: No, you can't go out again tonight. No, I don't want you getting involved in that. No, that costs too much money. No, you're too young to date…or go out with that group…or be with that guy that many times in one week.

And don't forget, if he needs a helping hand and asks you to do something, the answer's the same as to Mom—"Sure!"

As with Mom, your dad needs prayer. It's not easy being the leader of a family, a dad, and a provider for the family through his job.

Now, how about your brothers and sisters? First of all, if you have siblings, be thankful for them. My husband grew up an only child and tells me it was a pretty lonely life. He always had to go outside to find someone to play with and to make friends.

When it comes to your siblings, there are three key roles you can play in their lives: Encourage them, help them, and pray for them.

Everyone, including your brothers and sisters, can use encouragement. All kids struggle with schoolwork and grades, as well as with making friends and getting along. And everyone can use a friendly word of encouragement from a sister who comes alongside them with cheerfulness. Everyone can use a "Way to go!" "Good job!" "Hang in there!" "You're the best!" "I'm so glad I'm your sister."

And don't forget to encourage one another in the Lord. Help your brothers and sisters with their memory verses. Ask them about their Sunday school lessons. Talk to them about their devotions. Let them know you are praying for them.

Everyone can also use a helping hand. Ask your brothers and sisters if there's anything you can do for them today, or "How can I help?" When they're stewing over their homework, late getting out the door, trying to learn their Bible verses for their Bible club meeting, lend a helping hand and an understanding heart. After all, you've been there! Be on the lookout for ways to help out. Everyone appreciates—and needs—a helping hand.

And, boy oh boy, does everyone need prayer! Think of the grandest thing you could ask God to do for your siblings. Do they need to know Christ? Then pray! Do they need to get along better with Mom and Dad? Then pray! Are they sad because they don't have a friend at school? Then pray! Are they trying to make an important decision, like whether or not to go to college, or which college? Then pray! Do you have a sibling who has a physical or learning disability? Then pray— fervently! Is one of your brothers or sisters in a doubtful relationship with a boyfriend or girlfriend? Then pray! The Bible tells us to "pray for each other" (James 5:16).

The place at home—Someday in the future you will probably be in your mom's position—the watcher over your own home and flock. That's a good reason to watch her and assist her at home now. You'll be light years ahead in possessing the how-to knowledge you will need to take care of a home and the people who live there. Once again, give thanks to God for your mom—and learn as much as you can now.

But in the meantime, you have your own "little home"— your place, your space, your room or part of a shared room. Yes, every girl has her place and her stuff to take care of. So own the responsibility, master the management of your space, and enjoy the results. Be proud of what you do and create.

We've already talked about taking care of your clothes. And you'll want to take care of the condition and order of your room as well. Whatever skills or equipment you need to keep it clean, ask Mom for help. Which products do you use? Ask Mom. How can you organize and store all your things—CDs, books, pictures, souvenirs, art and craft supplies, jewelry, makeup, hair supplies, schoolwork? You know what to do—ask Mom!

Here's a little something that will help you along the way as you watch over your place:

> If you open it, close it.
> If you turn it on, turn it off.
> If you unlock it, lock it up.
> If you break it, admit it.
> If you can't fix it, call in someone who can.
> If you borrow it, return it.
> If you value it, take care of it.
> If you make a mess, clean it up.
> If you move it, put it back.
> If it belongs to someone else, get permission to
>   use it.[1]

An Invitation to Beauty

Home? Housework? Parents and siblings?

I know all of this may not seem very inviting or sound at all exciting, but don't forget, your space is just that—yours. And it's definitely worth watching over, worth your time and attention. In other words, it's definitely worth managing. When it comes to home and family, the effort you put in "a little place" like your space and relationships at home is meaningful work, important work. It helps you today, and prepares you for your future someday-home. Managing it well is important to God.

Now, enjoy the beauty of serving in a little place, a little place…like home.

A Little Place

"Where shall I work today, dear Lord?"
And my love flowed warm and free.
He answered and said,
"See that little place? Tend that place for Me."

I answered and said, "Oh no, not there!
No one would ever see.
No matter how well my work was done,
Not that place for me!"

His voice, when He spoke, was soft and kind,
He answered me tenderly:
"Little one, search that heart of thine.
Are you working for them or ME?
Nazareth was a little place…
so was Galilee."[2]

Using your Bible, read through Proverbs 31:10-31. Then write out verse 27 here:

In your Bible, read Exodus 2:1-10. How would you describe Miriam's relationship with her mother?

And what do you see Miriam doing for her mother?

How would you describe Miriam's relationship with her baby brother, Moses? And what do you see her doing for her brother?

What do you like most about Miriam, and how can you be more like her?

What was the most exciting truth or information you discovered in this chapter?

How did this chapter challenge you to be a better manager—to make improvements and changes in your attitudes and actions toward the place and people at home?

18

A Crowning Chorus

Your Praise

"Her children arise and call her blessed;
her husband also, and he praises her:
'Many women do noble things,
but you surpass them all.'"

PROVERBS 31:28-29

Every girl has her dreams. She watches Cinderella movies, reads Sleeping Beauty stories—on and on her input goes of meeting and marrying her "one true love." It's hard to find a girl—young or old—who doesn't wish for, desire, and dream of her "happily ever after." Yes, she yearns to one day marry, have children, and a home of her own.

As you step into these two verses describing the Proverbs 31 woman's marriage and family, you are greeted with a chorus of praise coming from her children and her husband. The scene sort of reminds you of a celebration banquet. And one by one, this lady's children and then her husband rise up and praise her.

Although you are probably not married now, it's likely that you will be in the future. But go ahead take a peek at what "true love" looks like in a marriage and family. What goes around, comes around: The love given out by this mom and wife is given right back to her from her family, along with praise and appreciation.

Praise for Mom

First we hear from the children. We don't know how many there are in this scene or their ages. But we do know these children verbalized their love and appreciation for their mom. They spoke up and wanted to let the whole world know what a great mother she was. But the most important person they wanted to hear their praise was Mom herself.

What did they say? We can only guess. If you scan back through Proverbs 31:10-31, you'll be reminded of her efforts, her love, and her character qualities that made her an excellent mom—and wife.

But *you* don't have to wait for some kind of celebration to praise your mom. You can do it today! Right now! Don't wait until Mother's Day to let her know what she means to you. Don't wait until her birthday to tell her that her thousands of selfless acts of love were noticed and appreciated. She's pouring out her love to you every single day. There's not one reason you can't—and shouldn't—praise and thank her every day and simply say, "I love you, Mom. Thanks for all you do!"

Praise for a Wife

Now it's her husband's turn. We already know our Proverbs lady is an excellent mom. And now we see she's also an excellent wife. Along with his children, her husband speaks praises of her as well.

The grand finale begins as "her husband also [rises up]"

(verse 28). He shares his own words of tribute, praising his incredible wife for all she's done for him, his family, and his home. He is glad to lift a crowning chorus of praise for her many selfless works through the decades.

An Army of Virtuous Women

Hear how her husband praises her: "Many women do noble things" (verse 29). Knowing what a noble woman is and does (after all, he's married to one!), this grateful man recognizes that *many* are noble. He realizes there is an entire army of good women, women of strong character out there.

He also acknowledges that "many daughters have done *well*" (verse 29 NKJV). He admits that many have done virtuously, excellently.

And he's not done yet. Read on!

The Best of All!

This happy husband just can't hold back his praise. He goes on, remarking, "But you surpass them all." His wife is beautiful not only in God's eyes, but in his eyes too. He wants her and the whole world to know that "you surpass them all! You transcend them all! You far outdo them all! You are better than all of them!"[1]

In other words, he points out that while other women "do" worthily, his wife "is" worthy. Other women "do" their activities (and do them excellently), but he praises his wife because of her very character: She "is" excellent![2]

Comparing her to all the other virtuous women in God's army, he shouts that she is the noblest of women. Summing up his praise of her, he declares, "You are the best of all!"[3]

A Challenge from God

I hope you are encouraged by this good news—many have done well. Unfortunately, a lot of people discount and put down and dismiss the Proverbs 31:10-31 passage in the Bible and the woman described there. I've even heard some women refer to the woman portrayed in this passage as "the woman I love to hate." They say, "She's too perfect. No one could live up to her standard. She can't be real. Who would even want to be like her?"

And yet this man, her husband, says the opposite. Yes, she is one of many. But, he reports, his wife excels them all.

God's challenge—and His will—for you is that you be one of the many. That you pursue excellence and this Proverbs 31 woman's beautiful character qualities. That you follow in her most excellent steps.

A Kaleidoscope of Virtues

Including verses 28 and 29, for 20 verses now we've looked at this woman, wife, and mom's godly character qualities. In a way, she's like a kaleidoscope. As a child, did you ever have a kaleidoscope, a small cardboard tube with two flat plates at one end that are filled with brightly colored glass or plastic pieces? When you hold a kaleidoscope up toward a light, you can view a stained-glass pattern created by the colored shards as the light shines through them. Then, as you turn the kaleidoscope, the many jewel-toned pieces tumble and change positions, creating one magnificent design after another.

Well, that's what the woman who is beautiful in God's eyes is like. In Proverbs 31, God gives you a chance to view the many qualities and aspects that make up her multifaceted life.

As we've moved from verse to verse, from virtue to virtue, God has illumined the exciting beauty of her virtues. Each verse and each quality shines as if viewed through a kaleidoscope. Each turn—each quality—reveals a new exquisite pattern. The Proverbs 31 woman is truly a kaleidoscope of virtues!

And you, my sweet friend, are a kaleidoscope of virtues too! You don't have to be a certain age or married to be a woman of character. Today, wherever you are, and whatever you are doing, be a P31. Be devoted to God, to following Him, to blessing others and pursuing the many qualities you've discovered in Proverbs 31:10-31. You'll be exquisite, so very beautiful in His eyes…and a blessing to all who know you or cross your path.

A Question for the Future

Are you still wondering, "How does this all apply to me? I'm just a teen waiting to learn how to drive a car!"—please don't forget that the emphasis throughout this book is on virtues, on godly character, on who you *are*, and not on whether or not you are married or have children. God wants all of His women to be filled to overflowing with His beautiful traits— and that includes you!

As we noted earlier, everything is in due time. Right now God wants you to develop the character of that Proverbs 31 woman. Character is built one day at a time over a lifetime. And the journey to excellence in all things starts today. Then, tomorrow, you get up and build on yesterday's character. So here's the challenge: You work on your character a day at a time, and God will do the rest!

An Invitation to Beauty

Did you notice there is no "How to Be Beautiful—Inside and Out" section in this chapter? That's because I wanted to make this section—An Invitation to Beauty—be about you, about your beautiful heart on the inside, and about your beautiful works and good deeds to others, especially at home.

We are standing very near the top of the mountain of character qualities we began climbing almost 20 verses ago. But before we take our final step or two, take a look at God's checklist for beauty:

As a young woman—Put the power of your mind and body to work to help others. Don't just *do* worthily. Be sure to *be* worthy.

As a daughter—Be a blessing to your parents. Honor them, do what they say, and make sure you contribute positively to the atmosphere at home.

As a sibling—Always encourage your brothers and sisters. Life is tough, so look for ways to be a strong source of support—their #1 Fan and their #1 Encourager.

Hopefully these are the desires of your heart. If that's true, you will grow even more beautiful inside and out as you pursue God's values. With His help and by staying on your toes, you can do it. You can be an excellent young woman, an excellent daughter, and an excellent sister. You can be beautiful in God's eyes…and I'm pretty sure in your parents' and siblings' eyes too!

Study Questions

Using your Bible, read through Proverbs 31:10-31. Then write out verses 28-29 here:

Another woman in the Bible was referred to as excellent or virtuous or noble. Read Ruth 3:11.

— How is Ruth referred to or described in your Bible translation?

—Who were the many voices praising her?

What does Proverbs 3:27 say about giving out to others what is good—praise, encouragement, thanks, as well as kindness and good deeds?

—Who does this verse say has the power to share these good things—or to withhold them?

—Make plans now to praise and bless your mom and dad. What will you do…and when?

What was the most exciting truth or information you discovered in this chapter?

How did this chapter challenge you to open your heart and mouth and praise your mom—and of course, your dad too?

19

A Spirit of Worship

Your Faith

"Charm is deceptive, and beauty is fleeting;
but a woman who fears the Lord
is to be praised."

Proverbs 31:30

You've done it! You've made it to your goal of making the climb we began in chapter 1. And I'm sending you a high five! As you look back and think, *Wow, I can't believe I've gone through nearly 20 of her character qualities,* you see you've come a l-o-n-g way. Now, finally, finally, in this book about beauty, we discover a verse that actually contains the word "beauty."

But wait a minute. What this verse says about beauty is probably not what you were expecting at the start. You've climbed toward the pinnacle of beauty...only to realize that it is not what you've been told all your life!

Here, just one verse short of the end of Proverbs 31, the message of Proverbs 31 comes into sharp focus, and you realize God's truth: What's important to a young woman is being beautiful not in people's eyes, not in the world's eyes, not in the media's eyes, not in an artist's eyes, but being beautiful in God's eyes.

And beauty in God's eyes is a totally different standard. God declares, "My thoughts are not your thoughts, neither are your ways my ways...As the heavens are higher than the earth, so are my ways higher than your ways and my thoughts than your thoughts" (Isaiah 55:8-9). In Proverbs 31:30 we have God's specific thoughts on beauty: "Charm is deceptive, and beauty is fleeting; but a woman who fears the LORD is to be praised."

As we near the end of our journey to discover God's take on beauty, you already know at least 19 of God's standards for your life as a woman. Now the mother teaching Proverbs 31 to us and her young son speaks again. Here she tells you exactly what is—and is not—beautiful in a woman.

The Twin Vanities of Charm and Beauty

"Charm is deceitful," Proverbs 31:30 declares.

Warning her son (and all who will listen), we can imagine this mother explaining, "Don't desire what is charming. Don't fall for charm. It is deceitful. It's fickle. It's fleeting. In the end, charm is one of life's illusions, one of life's vanities."

Charm may indeed lure you and fascinate a person, but it can never produce happiness, and it can never get the work of life done.

"And beauty is fleeting," she adds.

Still sounding the alarm, our teacher continues with her second warning: "And don't be fooled by looks. Remember that beauty is only skin deep. Beauty is vain, fleeting, fading—nothing but a vapor."

Sure, everyone appreciates physical beauty, but it is short-lived. It's temporary. And charm, beauty's twin sister, in no way guarantees a happy life. Neither beauty nor charm can help manage the nuts-and-bolts realities of life.

A Love for the Lord

This has been a awesome journey. We've looked at the beautiful character qualities of the Proverbs 31 woman. We've noted the many activities that fill her busy life. We've looked at her the same way we look at a watch—we've examined her moving hands and considered their message to us.

But here in verse 30 we are allowed a glimpse inside her so we can see what makes her tick. This woman is so amazing that we can't help but wonder: Where does her love come from? What's the source of her selflessness...her mercy...her incredible energy? What is it that guides her? What gives her purpose? And what defines her goals?

Our questions keep coming: What makes it possible for this woman to be such a solid rock? Where does she find the motivation to give herself to so many noble efforts?

And finally, what makes her so beautiful in God's eyes?

The answer is right here in verse 30. It is the final step in understanding God's beauty in her—it's the key. And God makes it crystal clear: It is God Himself. Verse 30 simply states, "A woman who fears the LORD is to be praised." She's beautiful inside and out because she loves Him. She "fears the LORD." She takes God seriously. And she takes obedience to His Word seriously too. God finds her love for Him beautiful.

A Heart That Loves the Lord

Are you wondering what it means to "fear" the Lord? It can sound pretty scary! But, in simple terms, a woman who fears the Lord is a woman who loves the Lord and has made a for-real, genuine spiritual commitment to Him.

And the good news is that it's totally possible for you to nurture this kind of love for the Lord. You can grow more beautiful inside as you focus more on your inner character and less on your outer appearance. You can steer your attention away from the clothes you wear or the hairstyle you choose, and focus instead on developing the character qualities God wants to see in you.

What difference does such a deep commitment to the Lord make? The simple answer: It influences all that you do! Everything in your life is affected when God is #1 in your life. Just as the sun radiates its light, the presence of the Lord shines through in all you do.

As a young woman whose heart is rooted in God, you will positively influence and minister to the people around you. Your conduct, your character, and your love for others will reflect the Lord and bless others.

How to Be Beautiful—Inside and Out

You already know that "a woman who fears the Lord is to be praised." And here's something else you probably already know: "The fear of the Lord is the beginning of knowledge" (Proverbs 1:7). The key to being beautiful on the inside is to fear (or love) the Lord. Here are a few how-to's for growing a deeper love for God.

1. "More Love to Thee, O Lord"—This is the title to a hymn that says a lot about your life's purpose and passion.[1] More love for the Lord should be a daily goal. You live out your fear of the Lord through your relationship to God's Son, Jesus Christ. This means the greatest question to you is, "Do you know Jesus Christ as your Savior and Lord?" Your faith in Him is the starting point to possessing the beauty of Christ.

2. Schedule time with the Lord—It's natural to spend time with a good or best friend, someone you really like. Well, it's no different when it comes to building a closer relationship and friendship with Jesus. So, like you do with your friends, make sure you spend lots of time with Jesus. You get together with your friends at school, church, sleepovers, after-school activities, or shopping. So get together with Jesus. Schedule a special get-together with Him every day.

Take a look at your schedule. You'll probably see school activities like exams and due dates for turning in your papers. Beyond school, you've got lessons to attend, practice time for instruments and performances, sports, and competitions, dental and orthodontist appointments. Oh, and then there's the fun stuff—birthday parties, sleepovers, ballgames, your Bible club or Bible study at church, even attending your brother or sister's events.

So here's the big question: Is "The Most Important Thing in the World" on your schedule? Is time with God written in on your daily schedule—in ink? When are your appointments with the Lord? Schedule time to be with Him, to learn more about Him as you read His Word and talk to Him through prayer?

Your faith in God strengthened when you take your Bible in hand and slip away to read it and pray. You've read a lot in this book about time management, organization, goals, and scheduling. So now it's time to use these lessons and skills. Put them to work for you to ensure that you spend life-giving, life-changing, life-beautifying time with the Lord.

3. Own God's plan—So many women wonder, "What is my purpose in life? What is God's plan for me?" Well, here's some great news! Proverbs 31 lays out God's plan for your life—a plan you can buy into. Sure, some details in your life will be different due to a 3000-year gap in history. But nothing can ever change the fact that God calls you to be a woman of character. Noble character. Godly character. Christlike character. And He wants you to embrace His plan and to own it. A woman who fears the Lord is a woman who is serious about God, about His Word, and about His plan.

4. Do your best—We don't know what the woman of Proverbs 31 looked like physically, but we have sure evidence that she did her best. And you too can—and need to—do your best. Here's how one author of our day approached God's plan for His women—including you. Author Anne Ortlund came to this conclusion:

> I noticed that twenty-two verses [of Proverbs 31] describe this woman's kindness, godliness, hard work, loving relationships—and only one verse out of the twenty-two [verse 22] describes how she looked [her clothing]…Seeing this kind of proportion in Proverbs 31…I prayed, "O Father, I want to give 1/22 of my time to making myself as outwardly beautiful as I can; and I want to give all the rest of my time, 21/22 of my life, to becoming wise, kind, godly, hard-working, and the rest."[2]

Not a bad formula, is it? Now figure out for yourself a way to nurture more love for the Lord and spend more time with Him. When you do, you'll have a formula for true beauty— real beauty—the beauty of your soul.

An Invitation to Beauty

In case you're not sure about how to have a relationship with Jesus Christ, let me invite you to make that relationship real today. Once you belong to Christ you can instantly begin living a life of true internal, eternal beauty! Consider praying these words now:

> Jesus, I know I am a sinner, and I want to repent of my sins and turn to follow You. I believe that You died for my sins and rose again victorious over the power of sin and death. I want to accept You as my personal Savior. Come into my life, Lord Jesus, and help me follow and obey You from this day forward.

I'm praying for you right now. True beauty begins in Jesus Christ.

Study Questions

Using your Bible, read through Proverbs 31:10-31. Then write out verse 30 here:

Look in your Bible at the scriptures below that show you some things God says about growing a heart that loves the Lord and how to be beautiful inside and out. Write a brief sentence about what these verses tell you to do:

"The fear of the Lord"—2 Peter 3:18:

"More Love for Thee, O Lord"— Philippians 3:20:

Schedule time with the Lord—Mark 1:35:

Do your best—Colossians 3:23:

What do these verses reveal about what a relationship with Jesus can—and will—do for you?

2 Corinthians 5:17—

John 3:15—

Philippians 4:13—

What was the most exciting truth or information you discovered in this chapter?

How did this chapter challenge you to grow in your devotion to God?

20

The Harvest of a Lifetime

Your Reward

*"Give her of the fruit of her hands,
and let her own works praise her in the gates."*

PROVERBS 31:31 (NKJV)

he way up is down." This is a modern-day "proverb" that sums up the path of the Christian life. And a look back at the Proverbs 31 woman's way of living shows us this kind of life. Day by day this lady served others and honored God. Keep this saying in mind as you now consider verse 31, the final verse in Proverbs 31. This verse is a magnificent summary of not only chapter 31 but of the entire book of Proverbs. I think you'll agree that, for our P31 woman, the Proverbs 31 woman, the way up was down.

Think about it. The woman who is beautiful in God's eyes, whose life and work we've been looking at for 22 verses in the Bible and 20 chapters in this book, has chosen to live her life in the shadows and to bear fruit that grows only in the shade.

At home, where few people see, she gives her utmost for God—she lives her days as a woman who fears the Lord (Proverbs 31:30). Oh, she does things—lots of things—outside as well. But, as we've said before, "What you are at home is what you are." Inside where Ms. P31 lives, there's no task too meaningless or effort too small to call for her most excellent endeavor.

Now, in verse 31, we see the rewards that await the woman who has been content to serve silently. A loud and unanimous chorus of praise is lifted for the woman who chose the way down.

The Fruit of Her Hands

Let's back up a minute and revisit the scene taking place in Proverbs 31. We see a mom. And we see a young prince, Lemuel. Lemuel's mother is using the Hebrew alphabet to help him remember what kind of woman he should look for as his wife.

As this mother ends her alphabetical poem, she gives her son one more word of instruction: "Give her of the fruit of her hands" (Proverbs 31:31). She explains that, just as admirers award conquerors with prizes for their heroic achievements that required strength, courage, and skills, so we too are to give God's beautiful woman her prizes, her rewards.

Paraphrased in today's words, Proverbs 31:31 could read, "Give her credit for her achievements. Give her all that she has earned! Give her all that she has worked for so diligently. Give her the fruit of her hands, the harvest of a lifetime of loving effort. Give her the profit she's earned, the goods she's worked, the reputation she's established, the marriage she's nurtured, the home she's built, the family life she's cultivated, the future she's labored for! Give it all to her."

Wow. You and I need to join in this chorus of praise too. We've seen this woman's heart, her character, her tireless efforts, her hands-on care for people. We too are being called by these final words to give the woman who is beautiful in God's eyes her rewards—a harvest of praise.

Unfortunately, some women today refer to the Proverbs 31 woman as "mousy," a wallflower, "just a housewife," a cave woman, and a slave. Some are quick to say, "Look at all her talent—it's such a shame it's wasted at home! Think how far she could rise in the corporate world with her abilities. Poor thing…what a waste!"

By now you know this kind of thinking could not be further from the message that God and His beautiful woman are sending to you. In fact, as one scholar says, "This verse forms a fitting conclusion to what is the most remarkable exposition in the Old Testament on the position of women, exalting…her functions in the home as wife, mother, and [manager]." This scholar's description goes on, ending with a final reference to the Proverbs 31 woman as "queen of the hearth."[1]

No, far from pitying this ideal woman, God calls you to praise her, admire her, study her, and follow her—especially to become her. You see, as a woman who fears the Lord, she shall be praised (Proverbs 31:30)—and that includes you!

Praise in the Gates

Proverbs 31:31 continues with a universal call to praise: "Let her own works praise her in the gates" (NKJV). These words are actually a twist to what was stated in verse 23…only that verse was about Ms. P31's husband. Verse 23 states, "Her husband is respected at the city gate, where he takes his seat among the elders of the land." In this verse, the spotlight is turned on her husband's prominent position in the gates of the city as a lawyer and leader.

Well, we now receive information that lets us know that his wife also has a position of honor in the gates. Other people are talking about her in public places. They are praising her for her many good works. In fact, "her own works" actually find a voice and "praise her in the gates" too.

And all of this is occurring "in the gates"—the place where people meet and congregate and talk, where matters of the law are settled and important announcements are proclaimed. Just think—after all she does so selflessly day in and day out, day after day and year after year, her praise is sung in public and the highest honor ascribed to her!

We've seen her willingly doing behind-the-scenes work. We've watched her do work that no one sees and goes unnoticed…or so we thought! Here we learn that her deeds are publicly acknowledged and acclaimed. Like her husband, she is known for her good reputation and solid character. She too has a high standing in the community.

It's true that many of her activities occur at home, yet her contribution to the community is given due recognition publicly in the gates. As one person notes, "Much of what… women do is in a supportive role, but imagine what would happen to a building if its support pillars were removed!"[2]

Young Lemuel's mother got it right. She says, "Let her own works praise her." Even if all voices were silent, even if no words of praise were ever spoken, the woman who is beautiful in God's eyes would receive the honor due her. How? The works of her hands and the fruit of her labor find a voice and proclaim her praise.

As our poem declares in verse 29, "A woman who fears the LORD, she shall be praised" (Proverbs 31:30 NKJV)—no matter what.

An Invitation to Beauty

What an incredible harvest of praise! We know this Proverbs 31 woman's husband and children praised her. And we know the people praised her. And we know her good works and deeds praised her. But the very fact that this verse—verse 31—is in the Bible means God is praising her too.

Oh, and did you notice there is one voice you *don't* hear praising her? It's her own voice! This sterling lady has no need to brag on herself, to blow her own horn, to shout from the rooftops, to point out all she's done. Her works are a result of her character qualities—God's kind of qualities. Her tireless, selfless works are what she's all about. As another proverb tells us, "Let someone else praise you, and not your own mouth; an outsider, and not your own lips" (Proverbs 27:2).

Now before we leave this book, and this fascinating, and stimulating, and encouraging, and motivating study of the Proverbs 31 woman, there's one more voice we need to hear—*your* voice!

Please don't buy into the world's view of this woman. I'll be honest: This woman and these verses in the Bible are not always appreciated by our culture. Our enemy Satan and the fallen world in which we live have rejected her beauty as being undesirable, unimportant, and even useless. Yet God chose to spend 22 verses in the Bible pointing you to her and praising her.

If you think about it, she is genuinely worthy of praise. To repeat, God is praising her here in the Bible. Her husband has praised her. Her children praised her. And all the people in the gates of the city praised her. Oh, and I'm praising her!

And now for you, my friend, as you continue on your way with God and grow more and more beautiful inside and out, don't forget to start now, today, whatever your age to...

— live what God's Proverbs 31 woman models. Mimic her. Follow her example. After all, she is God's ideal woman.

— consult her. When you have a problem, or a decision to make, or need a role model, revisit these 22 verses. Just curl up on your bed or favorite chair, get settled, open your Bible, and take a fresh peek at God's P31 lady. Ask "How would the P31 woman handle this problem, this issue?"

— return to her regularly. When you need encouragement as a young woman who's in the throes of growing up, return to her. As you read from Proverbs 31 again, God's "virtuous" or "noble" or "excellent" woman will go to work on your heart. She will inspire and instruct and encourage you when you fail.

So whenever you find your vision for your life and God's purpose for you dimming, the faithful life and dazzling character of the Proverbs 31 woman will infuse you with new energy. She will give you a fresh desire to live out God's purposes for you as a woman.

Study Questions

Using your Bible, read through Proverbs 31:10-31. Then write out verse 31 here:

Look at the table of contents at the beginning of this book and note the character qualities each chapter describes. Then list three qualities you want to get to work on right now—or know you need to get to work on right now. Then go ahead and write down the first step you will take toward building each character quality.

—

—

—

What messages do the following proverbs send to your heart about the beauty and value of hard work?

Proverbs 14:23—

Proverbs 27:18—

Proverbs 28:19—

Proverbs 31:31—

What was the most exciting truth or information you discovered in this chapter?

How did this chapter help you to determine the qualities you would like to be noticed for and receive praise for?

Notes

Chapter 1—A Sparkling Jewel
1. See Proverbs 14:30; 19:2; 19:11; 25:28.
2. See Proverbs 10:19; 15:28; 16:21,24; 31:26.

Chapter 2—A Solid Rock
1. Cheryl Julia Dunn, *A Study of Proverbs*, Master's thesis (La Mirada, CA: Biola University, 1993), 27.
2. Dunn, *A Study of Proverbs*, 27.

Chapter 3—A Spring of Goodness
1. Merrill F. Unger, *Unger's Bible Dictionary* (Chicago: Moody Press, 1972), 313.

Chapter 4—A Fountain of Joy
1. James M. Freeman, *Manners and Customs of the Bible* (Plainfield, NJ: Logos International, 1972), 198.
2. W.O.E. Oesterley, *The Book of Proverbs* (London: Methuen & Company, 1929), 284.
3. C.F. Keil and F. Delitzsch, *Commentary on the Old Testament—Vol. 6* (Grand Rapids: William B. Eerdmans, 1975), 329.
4. See verses 13,18,19,21,24.
5. G.M. Mackie, *Bible Manners and Customs* (Old Tappan, NJ: Fleming H. Revell, n.d.), 59.
6. Cheryl Julia Dunn, *A Study of Proverbs*, Master's thesis (La Mirada, CA: Biola University, 1993), 38.
7. Mackie, *Bible Manners and Customs*, 667.
8. Mackie, *Bible Manners and Customs*, 667.

Chapter 5—An Enterprising Spirit
1. Curtis Vaughan, ed., *The Old Testament Books of Poetry from 26 Translations—Lamsa* (Grand Rapids: Zondervan, 1973), 630.

Chapter 6—A Plan for Your Day

1. Alan Lakein, *How to Get Control of Your Time and Your Life* (New York: Signet Books, 1974), 46.

Chapter 7—There Is Profit in All Labor

1. *Webster's New Collegiate Dictionary* (Springfield, MA: G. & C. Merriam, 1961), s.v. "visionary."

Chapter 8—A Go-Getter Attitude

1. Curtis Vaughan, *The Word—The Bible from 26 Translations, A New Translation of the Bible,* by James Moffat (Gulfport MS: Mathis Publishers, 1991), 1250.

2. Cheryl Julia Dunn, *A Study of Proverbs,* Master's thesis (La Mirada, CA: Biola University, 1993), 64.

3. Curtis Vaughan, ed., *The Old Testament Books of Poetry from 26 Translations—Knox* (Grand Rapids: Zondervan, 1973), 630.

Chapter 9—A Taste of Success

1. Ted W. Engstrom, *The Pursuit of Excellence* (Grand Rapids: Zondervan, 1982), 36.

Chapter 10—A Little Night Work

1. Sybil Stanton, *The 25 Hour Woman* (Old Tappan, NJ: Fleming H. Revell, 1986), 169.

Chapter 11—A Helping Hand

1. Cheryl Julia Dunn, *A Study of Proverbs,* Master's thesis (La Mirada, CA: Biola University, 1993), 36.

2. David Thomas, *Book of Proverbs Expository and Homiletical Commentary* (Grand Rapids: Kregel, 1982), 793.

Chapter 12—An Eye on the Future

1. Curtis Vaughan, ed., *The Old Testament Books of Poetry from 26 Translations* (Grand Rapids: Zondervan, 1973), 631.

2. Vaughan, ed., *The Old Testament Books of Poetry from 26 Translations,* 631.

3. Robert L. Alden, *Proverbs: A Commentary on an Ancient Book of Timeless Advice* (Grand Rapids: Baker, 1990), 221.

Chapter 13—A Man of Influence

1. George Lawson, *Proverbs* (Grand Rapids: Kregel, 1980), 883.

2. Donald Hunt, *Pondering the Proverbs* (Joplin, MO: College Press, 1974), 432.

3. Elizabeth George, *Cultivating a Life of Character—Judges/Ruth* (Eugene, OR: Harvest House, 2002), 129.

Chapter 14—A Dream to Pursue
1. "Martha Stewart, Inc.," *Los Angeles Times Magazine*, August 2, 1992.

Chapter 15—A Wardrobe of Virtues
1. Robert Boyd Munger, *My Heart—Christ's Home*, rev. ed. (Downers Grove, IL: InterVarsity Press, 1986), 13, 15.
2. Cheryl Julia Dunn, *A Study of Proverbs*, Master's thesis (La Mirada, CA: Biola University, 1993), 126.
3. NASB.
4. NIV.

Chapter 16—A Law of Kindness
1. Charles Caldwell Ryrie, *The Ryrie Study Bible* (Chicago: Moody Press, 1978), 938.
2. Bill Crowder, *Daily Bread*, Kindle/ereader app. 7/17/13 regarding Psalm 19:14.
3. Crowder, *Daily Bread*, 7/17/13.
4. William MacDonald, *Enjoying the Proverbs* (Kansas City, KS: Walterick Publishers, 1982), 86.

Chapter 17—A Watchful Eye
1. Roy B. Zuck, *The Speaker's Quote Book* (Grand Rapids: Kregel, 1997), 174.
2. This poem has been adapted by others from the original poem attributed to Meade McGuire

Chapter 18—A Crowning Chorus
1. Curtis Vaughan, ed., *The Old Testament Books of Poetry from 26 Translations* (Grand Rapids: Zondervan, 1973), 632-33.
2. Cheryl Julia Dunn, *A Study of Proverbs*, Master's thesis (La Mirada, CA: Biola University, 1993), 163.
3. Kenneth Taylor, *The Living Bible* (Wheaton, IL: Tyndale, 1971).

Chapter 19—A Spirit of Worship
1. Lyrics by Elizabeth Prentiss (1856), music by William Howard Doane (1832–1915).
2. Anne Ortlund, *The Disciplines of the Beautiful Woman* (Waco, TX: Word, 1977), 46.

Chapter 20—The Harvest of a Lifetime
1. W.O.E. Oesterley, *The Book of Proverbs* (London: Methuen & Company, 1929), 283.
2. July Hubbell, *Messenger*, November 1975, 31.

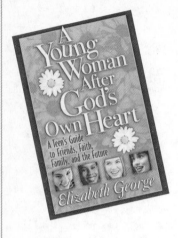

A Young Woman After God's Own Heart

What does it mean to pursue God's heart in your everyday life? It means understanding and following God's perfect plan for your friendships, your faith, your family relationships, and your future. Learn how to…

- grow close to God
- enjoy meaningful relationships
- make wise choices
- become spiritually strong
- build a better future
- fulfill the desires of your heart

As you read along, you'll find yourself caught up in the exciting adventure of a lifetime—that of becoming a woman after God's own heart!

A Young Woman After God's Own Heart
is available at your local Christian bookstore
or can be ordered at:

www.ElizabethGeorge.com

Other Great Books for Young Women
by Elizabeth George

A Young Woman's Walk with God
Love, joy, peace, patience, kindness, goodness, faithfulness, gentleness, and self-control are qualities Jesus possessed—and He wants you to have them too! Elizabeth George takes you step by step through the fruit of the Spirit to help you get the most out of your life. By paying attention to your journey with God, you'll be able to be positive as you interact with your family and friends, have peace regardless of the pressures of school and relationships, experience joy even when facing difficulties, find the strength to come through on your commitments, and gain control over bad habits.

As you walk with Jesus, your life will be more exciting and fulfilling every day...in every way.

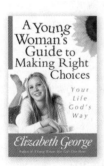

A Young Woman's Guide to Making Right Choices
You pick your clothes, friends, and boyfriends. You decide what to do and how to act at school, at home, and at the mall. You opt to do homework and chores. You also deal with temptations such as lying, cheating, drugs, and sex.

So what's the best way to handle so many options? Elizabeth shares verses and principles from God's Word that give you sure and easy ways to make the right decisions...the *best* decisions. This book will help you avoid trouble and bad situations, improve your friendships, develop confidence and character, get along better with your family, and set standards for your friendships with guys.

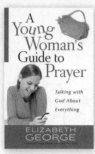

A Young Woman's Guide to Prayer

God wants to hear from you—yes, you! That's why He has given you an amazing gift—a way to talk things over with Him every day. Through prayer, you can tell Him all about your joys and triumphs, the hurts and fears you face, and your dreams and responsibilities, knowing that He cares about every single detail about your life.

In this practical book, Elizabeth George will help you grow a for-real relationship with God, make time to talk to Him, share your difficult situations and problems with Him, use prayer to guide you in making the right choices, and learn to trust God with every area of your life.

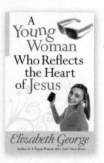

A Young Woman Who Reflects the Heart of Jesus

As you grow up, life gets more exciting, more fun… and more challenging. So much more to do, so many more choices to make. How can you consistently do what is best—and avoid making bad mistakes—at every step of the way?

Let Jesus show you. He's the perfect example for how to handle life. From Him you'll learn 12 character qualities that can make every area of your life so much better.

As you make Jesus' character traits your own, you'll discover better ways to handle daily life, experience joy, have great relationships with others, and enter into the thrilling journey of getting to know more and more about Jesus.

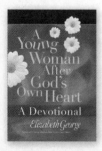

A Young Woman After God's Own Heart—A Devotional

In this devotional Elizabeth shares the best of *A Young Woman After God's Own Heart, A Young Woman's Call to Prayer,* and *A Young Woman's Walk with God.* You'll enjoy these short, dynamic, practical messages that build good habits, cultivate can-do attitudes, and fan the flames of passion for God.

Books by Elizabeth George

- Beautiful in God's Eyes
- Breaking the Worry Habit...Forever
- Finding God's Path Through Your Trials
- Following God with All Your Heart
- The Heart of a Woman Who Prays
- Life Management for Busy Women
- Loving God with All Your Mind
- Loving God with All Your Mind DVD and Workbook
- A Mom After God's Own Heart
- A Mom After God's Own Heart Devotional
- Moments of Grace for a Woman's Heart
- One-Minute Inspiration for Women
- Quiet Confidence for a Woman's Heart
- Raising a Daughter After God's Own Heart
- The Remarkable Women of the Bible
- Small Changes for a Better Life
- Walking with the Women of the Bible
- A Wife After God's Own Heart
- A Woman After God's Own Heart®
- A Woman After God's Own Heart® Deluxe Edition
- A Woman After God's Own Heart®— Daily Devotional
- A Woman's Daily Walk with God
- A Woman's Guide to Making Right Choices
- A Woman's High Calling
- A Woman's Walk with God
- A Woman Who Reflects the Heart of Jesus
- A Young Woman After God's Own Heart
- A Young Woman After God's Own Heart— A Devotional
- A Young Woman's Guide to Prayer
- A Young Woman's Guide to Making Right Choices

Study Guides

- Beautiful in God's Eyes Growth & Study Guide
- Finding God's Path Through Your Trials Growth & Study Guide
- Following God with All Your Heart Growth & Study Guide
- Life Management for Busy Women Growth & Study Guide
- Loving God with All Your Mind Growth & Study Guide
- Loving God with All Your Mind Interactive Workbook
- A Mom After God's Own Heart Growth & Study Guide
- The Remarkable Women of the Bible Growth & Study Guide
- Small Changes for a Better Life Growth & Study Guide
- A Wife After God's Own Heart Growth & Study Guide
- A Woman After God's Own Heart® Growth & Study Guide
- A Woman's Call to Prayer Growth & Study Guide
- A Woman's High Calling Growth & Study Guide
- A Woman Who Reflects the Heart of Jesus Growth & Study Guide

Children's Books

- A Girl After God's Own Heart
- A Girl After God's Own Heart Devotional
- A Girl's Guide to Making Really Good Choices
- God's Wisdom for Little Girls
- A Little Girl After God's Own Heart

Books by Jim George

- 10 Minutes to Knowing the Men and Women of the Bible
- The Bare Bones Bible® Handbook
- The Bare Bones Bible® for Teens
- A Boy After God's Own Heart
- A Boy's Guide to Making Really Good Choices
- A Husband After God's Own Heart
- Know Your Bible from A to Z
- A Leader After God's Own Heart
- A Man After God's Own Heart
- A Man After God's Own Heart Devotional
- The Man Who Makes a Difference
- One-Minute Insights for Men
- A Young Man After God's Own Heart
- A Young Man's Guide to Making Right Choices

Books by Jim & Elizabeth George

- A Couple After God's Own Heart
- A Couple After God's Own Heart Interactive Workbook
- God's Wisdom for Little Boys
- A Little Boy After God's Own Heart